# REFUGE
# and
# STRENGTH

GO PUAN SENG

PRENTICE-HALL, INC.
ENGLEWOOD CLIFFS, N. J.

*REFUGE and STRENGTH* by Go Puan Seng
© 1970 by Go Puan Seng

Library of Congress Catalog Card Number: 70-126825
Printed in the United States of America • *T*
ISBN 0-13-770503-4
Prentice-Hall International, Inc., London
Prentice-Hall of Australia, Pty. Ltd., Sydney
Prentice-Hall of Canada, Ltd., Toronto
Prentice-Hall of India Private Ltd., New Delhi
Prentice-Hall of Japan, Inc., Tokyo

*To*
**MARY BOYD STAGG**
**HAWTHORNE DARBY**
**HELEN WILK**
**MARTHA GARCIA AQUINO**
*Who*
*Gave Their Lives*
*That*
*Others Might Live*

# ACKNOWLEDGMENT

The author is most grateful to God and wishes here to record his appreciation to his daughter, Betty—the girl of seven who was with him in his exile—who worked all these years with him from the early manuscript to the final revision.

Sincere thanks are due Alfred E. Cain, senior editor of Prentice-Hall, for his discerning advice in the editing of the manuscript; to Shirley Hector, the author's representative, for her technical suggestions and cooperation; to publisher Joaquin P. Roces of the *Manila Times*, for giving the author access to the wartime records of the *Manila Tribune*; to Frederic H. Stevens, former President of the Philippine American Chamber of Commerce for his permission to use materials from his book, *Santo Tomas*; to Jean Edades, former head of the English Department of Arellano University, who enthusiastically went over the manuscript and contributed in no small part to the polish; to Lim Sian Tek, English editorial adviser of the *Fookien Times*; to Eduardo R. Sanchez of the *Financial Journal* and Juan E. Villasanta of the *Evening News* for their research work; to Rev. George Douma, for taking special interest in the author's early manuscript; to the United States Information Service publication, *Free World,* Rev. Oral Robert's magazine, *Abundant Life,* and the *Church Herald,* for publishing brief articles on the author's experience; and to his secretary, Elena N. Macalindong, for her untiring help in the preparation of the manuscript.

# FOREWORD *By* Norman Vincent Peale

Not in years has any book so moved and inspired me as has Go Puan Seng's *REFUGE AND STRENGTH*. It is actually a great human document of faith extraordinary, a quality of faith which even under the most terrible circumstances never once proved inadequate. It is not a theoretical book about the theology of faith, but rather a day-to-day documentation of the faith that never fails.

My friend "Jimmy" Go, publisher of the great Chinese language newspaper of the Philippines, the *Fookien Times,* was an aggressive opponent of Japanese expansion in the Far East. The writer of strong editorials and the orator at many public meetings opposing Japan's lust for power, when finally the Japanese attacked the Philippines Mr. Go was a marked man. He was the one person the enemy wanted to capture and destroy.

It was then that Mr. Go, with trusted companions, fled the city of Manila into exile in the rough mountainous country. For three years he and his family lived not unlike the beasts of the field, barely subsisting on berries and roots and wild fruit, and whatever could be smuggled to them by kindly friends. Always in imminent danger of capture; at times even within hearing of the voices of the enemy beating the brush in search of them. *REFUGE AND STRENGTH* thrillingly recounts the Providential nature of their protection and deliverance.

It was Mr. Go's faith that by reading the Bible he would be given practical and specific guidance concerning every move he should make. And almost hourly a decision had to be taken, a decision upon which hung the lives of his family, his fellow exiles, and himself. Sometimes the Bible guidance seemed to run counter to the judgment of his friends, but Mr. Go depended absolutely upon the Divine Word as he understood it, and followed it to the letter. Incredible preservation resulted.

An example of Mr. Go's use of the Biblical message to guide him and lead him through a multitude of dangers is the following experience:

"We were surrounded inside the Japanese General Yamashita's battle lines. That was in 1944, about the end of December, when the retreating Japanese soldiers were pouring into our mountains from the west side. By all human instincts, we should go East, run deeper into the mountains to keep distance between us and the retreating Japanese soldiers. We prayed to God, and God's answer was in the good book of Joshua. It said, 'Goeth down westward to the coast.' There were killings when people came face to face with the retreating Japanese soldiers. To go westward was surely to encounter them. But God said, 'Goeth westward.' When I told my group that we were going westward, many of them were against me. Some of them left me. Ten of them went east instead of westward. They never have returned. We followed God's answer. We followed God's guidance. We went westward. We did encounter Japanese soldiers retreating from the front but they did not do any harm. We also encountered quicksand in the battlefield. We saw one horse step in it, and the harder he struggled the deeper he sank. We detoured around the quicksand and continued our march westward until the sun went down. Finally and victoriously we came down from the mountains and reached the coastal city of Manila. In accordance with what God had said: 'Goeth down westward to the coast.' To human instincts it was impossible. To God it was the only way to safety. We prayed, we believed, we followed His guidance. God answered our prayers. He never failed."

As one follows the terrifying experiences of a few families in exile in the Philippine jungles and remembers that these were people of culture and position, the marvel of their adjustment to the rigors they suffered is impressive. Listening to Mrs. Go, a gentle lady of great refinement, at dinner in our home, tell in quiet voice of the hardship endured, one became aware that the power of faith in Christ can enable anyone to meet any crisis in this life.

*REFUGE AND STRENGTH*, written in the clear, succinct, forward-moving narrative style of a distinguished newspaper man, is one of the most thrilling adventure stories I have ever read. Indeed, I found it impossible to put the manuscript down, once I had begun to read. So fascinated was I by its amazing story, its astonishing demonstration of faith against overwhelming odds, that I set aside other responsibilities and gave myself completely over to the reading of this marvelous volume, not stopping until the glorious ending.

I warn you not to start reading this book unless you are prepared to follow it, as I did, to the end. You will be unable to let go of it; and so compelling is its interest that it will never let go of you. If you, the reader, will absorb even a small amount of "Jimmy" Go's faith, you will have a power over your problems greater than you have ever before experienced.

# CONTENTS

*I shall not die,*
*but live, and declare*
*the works of the Lord.*

**PSALM** 118:17

# CHAPTER ONE

❦

## THE INCREDIBLE HAPPENED

> *For behold, the darkness shall
> cover the earth, and gross dark-
> ness the people:*
>
> Isaiah 60:2

It was a February Saturday, just before high noon. The Philippine
tropical sun blazed high over our heads. Its rays cast a golden
glow over the multitudinous white marble crosses, strewn across
the gently sloping hillside of the Manila American Memorial,
creating a solemnity which made us feel serene and nostalgic.
Stately stretches of broad lawns with a great wealth of flowering
trees and plants, covering 142 acres, offered a quiet beauty, en-
hanced by the magnificent vistas of purple-tinted mountains far
beyond the mist, rising from the soft blue waters of Laguna de
Bay.

The Memorial, located within the army reservation of Fort
Andres Bonifacio, formerly Fort William McKinley, is situated
about six miles southwest of the center of Manila. The Philippine government granted permission to the American Battle Memorial Commission to build it. This memorial, erected after
World War II, is a proud remembrance of the sacrifices of the
soldiers from every state of the Union and the District of Colum-
bia, from Panama, Guam, Philippines, Puerto Rico, Australia,
Canada, China, England, Mexico, Costa Rica, Honduras, Fin-
land, Jamaica, Burma, and Peru.

Two extensive hemicycles embrace the Memorial Court.
There are inscriptions on the faces of its broad walls. Here are

*1*

recorded the names of some 36,279 U.S. armed forces including Philippine scouts who gave their lives in the service of their countries and who now sleep in unknown graves. Concentric circular rows of white marble headstones bearing the names of 17,182 U.S. military dead surround the outskirts of these hemicycles. A small devotional chapel stands nearby. Prayers, inset in gold tesserae on both sides of the blue glass mosaic walls, read:

> O God, who art the Author of peace and Lover of concord, defend us Thy humble servants in all assaults of our enemies that we surely trusting in Thy defense may not fear the power of any adversaries. Support us all the day long until the shadows lengthen and our work is done, then in Thy mercy grant us a safe lodging and a holy rest and peace at the last.

I had invited seventy-two-year-old General William C. Chase and his wife, Hallie, to view the Memorial with my wife, Felisa Velasco—whom I call Fely—and our youngest daughter, Grace, born after the war. They came to the Philippines on a sentimental journey. Twenty-five years ago, when the war was still on, Chase was sent by General Douglas MacArthur to recapture Manila in February 1945, and was known as its "Liberator."

We met two young American soldiers, a sergeant and his companion. They came to Manila for a four-day rest and recreation from war-torn Vietnam. The sergeant walked with dragging gait. He had only recently been released from the military hospital in Saigon. One could detect a thrill on the young soldier's face as he limped toward the elderly general. He introduced himself as the brother of a man who had once served in the army under the First Cavalry, of which General Chase was in command during World War II. His brother was killed in action on Philippine soil. This, of course, was the reason for this limping sergeant's visit to the Memorial.

In their brief conversation, after the young sergeant related the situation in Vietnam, we heard General Chase remarking,

2

"Each man, in his own generation, fights for his country." No doubt he took pride in the part he had played during World War II and was encouraging the two young soldiers to do their parts, too. The young soldiers were solemn. The scene before them must have affected them deeply.

We then came to the portion of the Memorial where the maps lay. There were 25 military maps done in mosaic and ceramics. As Chase studied the maps and followed with precision the course of the First Cavalry during those blitzkrieg days and nights of marching—through Norzagaray and Santa Maria in Central Luzon, to Manila—a beam on his face told us he was re-living those glorious days. Step by step we watched his eyes pore over those vertical rows of walls on which were carved thé names of those who had died in battle. His earnest look gave way to long-forgotten names of those who had fought under his command.

Norzagaray, where General Chase and his First Cavalry had pulled through to battle southward, was the hilly region where I had escaped into self-exile with my family and friends.

I, Go Puan Seng, a Christian Chinese, was a wanted man by the Japanese Occupation Army when the Philippines fell. I was then in my early thirties.

In the first week of December 1941, my newspaper had run a banner headline: "One Hundred Japanese Warships Heading for Philippine Waters, Rome Reports." When the desk editor showed it to me, I smiled at the thought of the boost this pre-posterous statement would give to the sales of that edition. "Things cannot be as serious as the report indicates," I said, never imagining that at that very moment the Japanese fleet had stolen to within striking distance of Pearl Harbor and that the invasion of the Philippines was imminent.

On December 7 our household was filled with joy. It was the day our two-year-old son, Andrew, was to be baptized. Four girls—Betty, aged seven, Cecilie six, Dorcie four, and Elsie three—had come first. We had named our children alphabetically. We had reserved "A" for the boy, our fifth child. For the first time, Andrew was dressed in a shiny sharkskin suit while his sisters looked gay in colorful cotton prints. It was a sunny morning. Our garden and the flowers that lined the driveway seemed gilded as we set forth in our new Mercury for the Chinese United Evangelical Church.

After the baptism we celebrated with a luncheon for close friends at the fashionable Great Eastern Hotel. As our happy gathering was about to end, Mrs. Mary Boyd Stagg, American pastor of the Cosmopolitan Student Church and sponsor for our son, casually asked, "The international situation looks rather bad; do you think war will reach the Philippines?" Mrs. Stagg probably thought that, being a newspaperman, I would know the answer.

Laughing confidently, I replied, "Should the Japanese be so stupid as to involve the Philippines in the war, the American Air Force with its 'flying fortresses' would annihilate Tokyo in two weeks' time." All our guests applauded my remark, and we noticed an officer of the USAFFE Air Force at a nearby table smiling and nodding. (General Douglas MacArthur, with headquarters in Manila, had been commissioned to organize the United States Armed Forces in the Far East, known as the USAFFE.)

But nothing is sure on this earth. As a Chinese adage has said,

> Just as the heavens may blow or cloud over, man
> may suffer or rejoice in one day's span.

That night the incredible happened. War broke out between Japan and the United States.

Bombs, released from Japanese planes that roared across our tropical skies, detonated day and night. Horror, anxiety, and suspense gripped the people. Enemy amphibious invasion activity soon began.

"The Japanese Army landed today at Ilocos and are on their way to Manila," exclaimed Carlos P. Romulo, then publisher

*4*

of the *Philippines Herald,* when I called on him at his newspaper office. Romulo had just returned from a tour of Southeast Asia and had written a series of articles on Japan's aggressive designs, for which he was later awarded the Pulitzer Prize.

We both knew that the Ilocos provinces, situated near the northern tip of Luzon Island, are separated from the Japanese base at Formosa only by a short stretch of sea. And from Ilocos to Manila runs a highway of but 383 miles. "You will be the first Chinese they'll shoot," Romulo jokingly warned me.

I was stunned!

# CHAPTER TWO

## PEARL OF THE ORIENT SEAS

> *Keep me, O Lord, from the hands*
> *of the wicked; preserve me from*
> *the violent man.*
>
> Psalm 140:4

Did Romulo consider my fate sealed because of my anti-Japanese activities?

From the day way back in 1931 that the Japanese set aflame (in conflagration) the northern barracks in Mukden, Manchuria, to their invasion of Shanghai, on to the incident of Lukouchiao in northern China which set Japan and China at war, my newspaper had all along advocated resistance against Japanese aggression and their encroachment of Asia. I was one of the main orators in the various mass meetings among the Chinese people in Manila. The metropolitan dailies, including Romulo's, called me the "fiery editor"; at times, they even addressed me as the "fighting editor."

I sponsored and directed boycotts against Japanese goods and was one of the founders of the Anti-Japanese Aggression League. Under me, a group of patriotic youths risked their security for the cause. They fought with influential traitor-suspects.

One afternoon I was beaten while passing a corner around the banking area on foot. The assailant had escaped. It could have been an act of retaliation from my opponents. With a bandaged head, immediately following the incident, I delivered impassioned speeches at a big rally at the Manila Grand Opera

House, vigorously attacking Japanese aggressors and Chinese traitors. The Chinese public took me to be a symbol of patriotism.

In fact, even before launching the boycott campaign, the Philippine cosmopolitan journalistic circle had already regarded me as a combative editor in my own domain. I had had the experience of a long court fight in a libel suit in defense of a slave girl against her master, and was sentenced by the lower court to two months' imprisonment. My stand, however, was upheld by the Supreme Court and my acquittal was hailed by all newspapers and celebrated as a victory of the freedom of the press. When the boycott movement was at its height, I came to face another court dispute. The City Fiscal's office had only recently dismissed a complaint against me filed by the Japanese Consul-General with the Commonwealth Government for allegedly insulting the Japanese emperor in my writings. It was beyond doubt that the enemy had marked me for liquidation.

Soon, Romulo quit his newspaper work to join the USAFFE.

Following the report that about 80 Japanese ships had been sighted off Lingayen Gulf in northern Luzon, came the announcement: "MacArthur Takes Field." The general had moved his headquarters to Bataan Peninsula, 77 miles southwest of Manila. And Manila was declared an open city.

Ignorant of the extent of the American loss in Pearl Harbor, the people still expected the momentary arrival of reinforcements from the United States. Men in the streets counted on a turn in the tide of the war not by days but by hours.

For my wife, the abrupt changes brought about by the catastrophe of war were almost too much to bear. "Why must peaceful homes be wrecked by war?" she prayed in her perplexity. My wife belongs to a Chinese family who had become Filipino citizens during the Spanish regime. Her great-grandfather, Mariano Velasco, was a most successful businessman in the late 19th and the early 20th century. A devout Christian since her childhood days when she attended kindergarten at the St. Stephen Girls School and then the Centro Escolar College in

Manila, she took the initiative in urging me to go to church during our courtship days. I was baptized and was given the Christian name James.

By heredity I belong to the third generation of a Buddhist family. By education I was steeped in the philosophy of Confucius. By profession I was a newspaperman, inclined, like most of my colleagues, to be a free thinker. By the love and grace of God, my wife had brought me to know Christ. But only after I had suffered tribulations did I begin to lose myself in the divine contemplation of a life reborn.

Since our marriage in 1932, blessed with five children, we enjoyed a fine family life. Manila then was a peaceful city. Naturally, Fely was not prepared for the horrors of war.

The Philippines was poetically called "Pearl of the Orient Seas" by its national hero, Dr. José P. Rizal. Barely 500 miles off the southeast rim of Asia, just outside its continental shelf, the Philippines is a cluster of over 7,000 islands extending some 1,200 miles from north to south and some 700 miles from west to east. The archipelago, composed of three big groups, Luzon, Visayas, and Mindanao, is bounded on the north by the Bashi Channel, on the south by the Celebes Sea, on the west by South China Sea, and on the east by the Pacific Ocean, a portion of which became known as the Philippine Sea. The largest and most populated island is Luzon in the north which is characterized by rugged mountain ranges and narrow fertile coastal plains. Manila, the capital city in the heart of Luzon, rises on the shores of Manila Bay, a natural basin for shipping, within a few miles of the foothills of the Sierra Madre mountains.

The archipelago, therefore, formed not only a natural entrepôt of the trans-Pacific trade but an intelligence outpost in Southeast Asia. Controlled by the United States, the archipelago was a barrier to Japanese imperial designs southward toward Indonesia and Australia.

The Filipinos are basically of Malay stock with strong influences from other peoples who have crossed the paths of Philippine history, notably Chinese, Indians, and Spaniards. From the coastal cities of South China, traders came to the islands during the Sung Dynasty (960-1279 A.D.) or even earlier during the Tang Dynasty (698-907 A.D.), living in harmony and mingling with the islanders and, through the years, joining the mainstream of Philippine life. A great number of Filipinos including Dr. José Rizal, who was executed by the Spaniards at the turn of the century, are descended partly from Chinese forbears.

Searching for a new route to the spice islands of the east, Ferdinand Magellan landed in southern Philippines in 1521 and inaugurated 400 years of Spanish domination of the archipelago—turning the Filipinos into Asia's only Christian nation—which ended in 1898 when the United States acquired the islands after the Spanish-American war. Filipinos had raised the banner of independence during that war, only to see themselves ceded to the U.S. by the Treaty of Paris.

America's half-century rule of the Philippines started an era which saw major strides taken in the fields of education, public administration, communications, and commerce, along with growing political maturity and nourishment of democratic and libertarian ideas among the people. The Philippines was then known as a melting pot of different races and the show window of democracy in the Orient. Independence, the goal of Filipinos during this period under the enlightened leadership of men like Manuel L. Quezon and Sergio Osmeña, Sr. had been promised. In 1936 a Commonwealth government largely autonomous in internal matters, with Quezon as President and Osmeña as Vice-President, in which General Douglas MacArthur served as military adviser, was formed to pave the way for independence. The people awaited the day. But their expectations were rudely shattered by the coming of the Japanese invaders from the north.

After my talk with Romulo, I called on another colleague, Roy C. Bennett, editor of the American-owned *Manila Daily Bulletin*. We agreed that the fall of Manila was but a matter of days. But we trusted in the promise of President Franklin D. Roosevelt, broadcast on Christmas Eve, that powerful help was on its way and that the Philippines would be redeemed.

*9*

"Redeem," usually a word to give courage, now had an ominous sound, suggesting an intervening period of agony.

"Sit tight inside the house," Roy advised me. "It won't be long."

He thought the enemy would respect international law as he himself would, and that though the city would be occupied, the enemy would still allow us to live there until the American forces returned.

To stay at home, waiting for the enemy to come, was to become a sure prey. I saw very little hope in Roy's suggestion.

I suspended publication of our newspaper, the *Fookien Times,* after the December 29th issue and disbanded its staff members. Sadly, I ordered our newspaper plant closed and bade farewell to my co-workers. I asked them to seek their own way out. The less they had to do with me, the safer they would be. "The Americans will come back as we will all come back," my old friend Vicente L. del Fierro said in parting, as he squeezed my hand.

The following night our home telephone rang. It was an urgent call from another associate, Ernesto del Rosario, who became editor of the *Manila Chronicle* after the war. "San Pablo has fallen," he shouted. San Pablo, a town about 45 miles southeast of Manila, is a gateway to the city. "Destroy all records of the paper, and you better beat it." In this great emergency Ernie had thought of me and our co-workers' safety.

I had to leave the city. And I could leave no clues to jeopardize my staff members.

# CHAPTER THREE

## FLIGHT AND CAPTURE

*Plead my cause, O Lord, with them that strive with me: fight against them that fight against me. Take hold of shield and buckler, and stand up for my help.*

Psalm 35:1-2

On the eve of the fall of Manila, loyalty and integrity were on trial. A large majority stood firm in their convictions, even as others prepared to court the graces of the invaders.

The Japanese used a pincer movement to capture Manila. Following their initial success at Ilocos and the landing of the bulk of their army at Lingayen Gulf, they attacked from the south. Fires and explosions all around us indicated that the Manila garrisons had started the demolition of military targets and supplies. At Pandacan, on the southern edge of the city and where gasoline and oil were stored, thick smoke surged upward, visible for miles. The city's black days had begun. The outnumbered USAFFE was in full retreat.

My wife started to prepare for our family's evacuation. Our children's dainty dresses were put away and their new clothes were made of navy-blue denim, which could better stand the strain of moving from place to place. Fely believed that as soon as the Japanese entered Manila, they would start tracking down their political foes. "You must run away while there is still time," she urged me with tears in her eyes.

"What about the family?" I asked.

"It would be hard for the whole family to keep up with you.

*11*

We will follow afterward whenever necessary," she replied. She insisted that the sooner I leave the city, the better would be my chance of escape.

I did not have the faintest idea where to flee. I had not planned before and I could not plan now.

But since leave I must, and at once, I thought of dashing through central Luzon to Bataan and joining the USAFFE as my colleague Romulo had done. Unfortunately, the military situation took a sudden turn. Before I could act, MacArthur ordered the disbandment of many divisions. He was reducing personnel instead of recruiting more. I was late.

I sent for my friend Yang Sepeng, who was the secretary of both the Philippine Chinese General Chamber of Commerce and the Anti-Japanese Aggression League. Yang, too, could be a wanted man. After brief deliberation, Yang decided to accompany me into hiding and to send his wife, Filomena Hernandez Barrameda, whom we called Eva, and his son, Arthur, to the dormitory of the Cosmopolitan Student Church, under the care of Mrs. Stagg. Yang, in his early thirties, had come to know the Staggs through me and had become a Christian.

Yang's willingness to join me lifted my spirits.

While we were planning our moves, a neighboring Chinese merchant, whom we called Tony, dropped in. He was several years my senior, an intelligent and active participant in the Anti-Japanese Aggression League.

"Are you planning to leave the city?" he asked.

"Yes, unless we choose to surrender. There is no other way," I answered.

"I have a small bottle of poison and always keep it with me. I plan to take it if the enemy forces me to surrender," Tony said. Apparently, he wanted to prove to us his firm conviction and to dispel whatever doubts we might have had about him. "If you have no objections, let me join you in your flight. I'll go wherever you go," Tony begged.

Tony thought I would be able to plan a wise escape. I told him truthfully we had no plan except to leave the city immediately.

"I will go home to get some clothes and will be back in no time," he said, suiting the action to the word.

Yang, too, rushed to his house to pack and promised to return with his car.

It was December 31, 1941, the birthday of our first daughter, Betty. She was born on a gay New Year's Eve seven years ago. Sunny and sweet, she had brought us much happiness.

I refused to leave without tasting the birthday noodles, which in Chinese tradition symbolize long life. I felt a big lump in my throat as I scooped up the noodles with my chopsticks. Overwhelmed by emotion, I left the table for my room, followed by my wife. Betty and her little sisters and brother looked after us with wonder.

Our parting was bitter and sad. Where lay our safety? When should we be united again?

The thought of leaving my aged mother and our children in the care of my wife at such a time tormented me. Everything seemed black.

My wife knelt with me in prayer, trusting in Psalm 84 that God would be my sun and my shield on my road to exile.

At one o'clock in the afternoon Yang and Tony arrived. My wife folded one linen suit into a big canvas bag already bulging with blankets, milk, oatmeal, crackers, and other food. The plan was for me to carry the knapsack and live in the jungle, sleeping under trees as we awaited the promised redemption.

Seeing their daddy about to leave, our children began to cry. We failed to sing "Happy Birthday" to dear little Betty. Beyond the small hill where our home stood, explosions reverberated.

"Son, when will you return?" my aged mother kept asking me. I could only look at her in reply.

"I give you unto the hands of our Heavenly Father," my wife said as she waved good-bye.

I left with a breaking heart.

Tony and I sat in Yang's car, with Yang at the wheel. The car was loaded with canned goods. We headed northeast, toward the hilly region.

"So this is the beginning of our hunted life," I said.

*13*

"From now on, whether we live or die, we are one," said Yang.

"Let us not forget one another if we come back alive," added Tony.

We had no idea where we were going. We had only a road map published by an oil company. The hilly region of Ipo in eastern Bulacan, one of the provinces near Manila, flashed through Yang's mind.

In early December, during the heavy Japanese bombing, Mrs. Stagg had thought of finding a place for a refugee camp for members of the church. Once she had taken Yang and other church members to explore Ipo, where a church member, Captain Serafin Aquino, owned some land.

Almost without thinking, Yang drove toward the Ipo valley. Crossing a bridge about 19 miles from Manila, we were surprised by a group of armed men in uniform. They swarmed out of the jungle and surrounded us.

"Where are you headed for? Don't you know the enemy is approaching us from the north?" barked the sergeant.

Before we could reply, a soldier shouted, "Hey, look at the road map which contains military information."

Tony had brought a pistol which he thought might be useful in jungle existence. Yang had two axes hidden in the car, and I had a bolo, a native all-purpose knife. The axes had eluded the soldiers' eyes, but they took the map, the gun, and the bolo as evidence and immediately arrested us. The armed men, seven in all, squeezed into the car and directed Yang to turn westward.

"Where are we going?" Yang asked.

"We have to take you to San Jose," answered the sergeant grimly. San Jose was a town in Bulacan province, a few miles away.

Yang had no choice but to follow the order.

"We caught two German spies yesterday and shot them right on the spot," a soldier remarked casually. He sat in the rear with Tony's pistol pointed at Yang's neck.

The jungle was deathly silent save for the shrill chirping of birds. A blue sky only made the scene more dismal by contrast.

We knew that if these soldiers became tempted by the foodstuffs and our personal belongings, they could easily do away with us in this no-man's-land. In such a deserted area no one could have come to our rescue. No information would have reached our families. Soon our bodies would have become prey to the birds and beasts of the jungle. And our fate would forever remain a mystery!

We were in a tight spot. We tried to explain, but it was futile. I showed the soldiers my press pass signed by Major Diller, press officer of MacArthur's headquarters. It allowed me to enter all theaters of war. They laughed it off.

"A good spy would equip himself with all the necessary credentials," retorted a soldier.

What irony! We had been taken to be spies of the very enemy from whom we were fleeing. Facing possible death, Tony murmured: "Would it not have been better to stay in the city and die like lions instead of being killed in the jungle like snakes?"

Yang was silent. Too late for regrets. What could save us? I could not think of anything.

"I give you unto the hands of our Heavenly Father"—the parting words of my dear wife rang clearly in my ears while I prayed silently.

# CHAPTER FOUR

❧❦❧

## CAPTAIN AQUINO TAKES COMMAND

> *Though I walk through the val-*
> *ley of the shadow of death, I will*
> *fear no evil: for thou art with me;*
> *thy rod and thy staff they comfort*
> *me.*
>
> Psalm 23:4

We drove on. Then the sergeant looked closely at me and suddenly began to speak in an understanding manner.

"I know you are good people, but it is my duty to take you to the municipality and make my report," he said and ordered his soldier to stop toying with the pistol.

What a relief it was!

Our car soon stopped in front of the municipal building.

News of our arrest spread like wildfire among the townsfolk, who crowded around us. They had been told that spies had been captured on their way to join the enemy in the north. Seeing us, most of them were convinced that the charges against us were exaggerated. The municipal mayor, however, insisted on enforcing military rules and keeping us in jail for the time being.

Conscious that he was responsible for our predicament, the sergeant, who had now realized his mistake and had become our friend, argued vainly in our defense.

"Airplanes! Airplanes!" the crowd at the plaza shouted. While the people scampered right and left for safety, the three of us—suspected spies—were left standing in the plaza. We

*16*

could not run away, for the municipal police might shoot us for attempting to escape.

The commotion gave us a few moments alone.

We feared not so much the airplanes above as the threat of jail below. The Japanese invaders were marching down from the north unopposed. They would soon reach Malolos, the provincial capital, and then this municipality. I had exposed my identity when I showed my press credentials to the soldiers and the municipal authorities. The moment the enemy knew who I was, we would either be taken prisoner or possibly be put before the firing squad.

Though foreseeing more troubles ahead, I refused to give up hope. My faith was sustained by the change of the sergeant's attitude.

The enemy planes passed over without doing any damage. As they disappeared in the distance, the chief of police came to take us to jail. He started to ask our names and our purpose in traveling through the region.

"We are going to Ipo to join the Aquino family," Yang replied calmly.

At the name "Aquino" a remarkable change came over the chief of police.

"Oh, the Aquinos. They are my friends!" he exclaimed.

He quickly sought the mayor and proposed to take us to Ipo with a guard to check with the Aquinos, for Captain Aquino was well-known to them.

The mayor was reluctant at first but finally agreed. "If your story is found to be false, you will be jailed," he warned as he pointed a threatening finger at us.

Who was Captain Aquino? I could not recall the name. Yang had visited Mrs. Aquino with Mrs. Stagg once, but he doubted whether she would recognize him.

The sun was setting when we reached a group of four or five houses. Among them was the Aquino home—a small, wooden structure facing the rocky, narrow Ipo highway. Captain Serafin Aquino, a reserve officer of the Philippine Army, was at the

*17*

battle front. An old dog barked at us suspiciously. Soon Mrs. Aquino came to the door, perturbed at this visitation from the chief of police, a uniformed guard, and three strangers.

She gazed at us anxiously for a moment, then smiled. "Oh, Mr. Yang and Mr. Go! What brought you here? What is the plan of the church? And what is the news from Manila?" A warm welcome. No sign of distrust. Her hospitality overwhelmed the officers, who quickly bade us good-bye.

"It is over," Yang remarked as we relaxed within the house, much relieved, though we knew this incident was but the prelude to more danger. Only that morning had we left home, but the fearful experiences packed into that one day were staggering to recall.

Evening fell; supper was ready. A solitary flickering candle lit up the table. Bagoong alamang—tiny reddish, salty shrimps, the best food available in those uncertain days—was served with a dish of plain rice.

For the first time I tasted bagoong. What a contrast to the birthday noodles and the delicious viands left untouched at our home! This was indeed the beginning of a changed life.

Tony and I could not eat, but Yang tried his best to please our hostess. We were weary but grateful to God that our lives had been spared. To breathe free air that evening among the peaceful hills was a benediction.

Enormous fires in the direction of Manila lit the sky and thunderous explosions rocked the night.

Mrs. Martha Garcia Aquino had many relatives living with her—her mother, "Impo"; her two sons, Serafin, Jr. and Ernesto; and five daughters, Rebecca, Elizabeth, Martha, Priscilla, and Amelia. Rebecca and Elizabeth were married, both their husbands being in the army. With them were Rebecca's children, Linda and Eddie, and Elizabeth's baby daughter, Ophelia. The house was very crowded.

The Aquinos had an elderly friend called Mang Juan, who lived on a farm with his family among other poor mountain folk a few miles deeper in the jungle. That night Mrs. Aquino and her elder daughters moved to Mang Juan's farm to allow space in her own house to accommodate us.

We stayed in the wooden house with Impo and the Aquinos' younger children. While the wind was furiously whipping the tall cogon, a voice suddenly called for night devotions. It was young Martha, whom we called "Baby."

"Our family always gathers and prays before going to bed," she said. With her sweet little voice of an angel, Baby reminded us of our spiritual needs in a world gone mad.

Thoughts of my family rushed into my tired mind. I wept as I prayed. Thus, Tony, Yang, and I spent our first night of self-exile in the strange hilly region.

Mrs. Aquino returned with Mang Juan at dawn. We had all forgotten that it was New Year's Day. None of us greeted the others with the usual New Year wishes.

Mang Juan and Mrs. Aquino thought the Japanese might send soldiers to guard Ipo Dam, with its reservoir, a few kilometers from the Aquino house. "It would be safer for you to move to my place, which can be reached only on foot," said Mang Juan.

Tony, who had been deeply affected by our arrest the day before, doubted Mang Juan's plan. He thought we should explore other possibilities before risking the hazards of the jungle.

But Mang Juan had schemed to keep us with him.

In the midst of our discussion, a boy rushed in shouting, "Japanese are coming!" Everybody was scared and started to run. We had no choice but to follow Mang Juan to his farm immediately. Later, we found it to be a false alarm.

In Ipo rain comes almost nightly. Streams, big and small, crossed the mountain paths. The trail was muddy and rocky. It was a new and hard experience for us—a two-hour hike and climb over rough terrain.

Mang Juan's nipa hut stood at the crossing of two mountain trails, and many passersby stopped there to gossip. There was no way of hiding our presence. Some looked at us with suspicion, while others referred to us with sarcasm.

At night we slept on the bamboo floor in the nipa hut, among strangers who had sought shelter with Mang Juan. Several dogs, who spread fleas freely, became our sleeping mates. Before long, we discovered to our dismay that our stock of canned goods had diminished faster than we had figured.

Fantastic rumors flew from mouth to mouth. "Manila has fallen. The Japanese Army has rounded up all the Chinese leaders and has chopped off their fingers," someone told Mang Juan.

The four days that we had been cut off from communication with Manila seemed years. The bridge where we had been arrested as spies had been dynamited on New Year's Eve, only a few hours after we had crossed it. The best way to reach Manila now was on horseback, following the mountain trails to Marikina Valley northeast of the city. We finally persuaded Mang Juan to make the trip and try to contact our families.

But the old man dared go only as far as the suburbs. He returned two days later, bearing a copy of the *Manila Tribune* published one day after I had left home. The front page carried a picture of the Manila City Hall with banner headlines quoting the chief of police's statement: "Open City—No Shooting," which meant that the Japanese troops were free to enter Manila, for there would be no resistance.

The occupation of Manila was certain.

As we digested this dread fact, we heard sobs and saw with a pang that Mrs. Aquino was crying. We attempted to comfort this brave and great-souled woman, but to no avail. The strain had been severe. We all felt the agony of utter helplessness.

That day Tony, Yang, and I wandered around the deserted hills. Dark clouds hung over us. Not a soul was in sight. The familiar swishing of the breeze through the cogon grass intensified our dejection.

"How can we go on like this?" Tony asked.

"What else can we do?" Yang countered. "We cannot get out of here without Mang Juan's help, and we cannot be sure of finding a safer place to run to."

We returned to Mang Juan's house for lunch. Suddenly the

faithful old dog Bruno barked, and we heard Mang Juan shout excitedly, "Compadre!" (This means godfather of my child or father of my godchild.) Captain Serafin Aquino stood before us, accompanied by a lieutenant. Mrs. Aquino and all her family wept for joy.

The Captain was a muscular and robust middle-aged man, self-confident and well-disciplined. His regiment had been disbanded before the fall of Manila, and he had hiked to Ipo.

His arrival was to help us out of our predicament, but at the time we three fugitives failed to understand this. At first we had doubted whether Mrs. Aquino would receive us. Next we had feared whether we could trust Mang Juan. Now we dreaded the attitude the Captain would take.

During lunch the Captain made an unexpected announcement. "The three of you must move to a new jungle hideout with me and my family as soon as I can put up a camp," he declared, pointing to Tony, Yang, and me. He told Mang Juan that since we were his guests, he was responsible for our safety.

Mang Juan was astonished at these abrupt words.

On the very next day Captain Aquino took his family and relatives away from Mang Juan's place, leaving us to make up our minds.

The Captain was obviously a more dependable leader, but under the circumstances we could not afford to displease Mang Juan. We had lost confidence both in ourselves and in others. We lingered for two more days, vacillating.

"Sooner or later we've got to move out of here," Tony remarked.

"And the sooner the better," Yang added.

We all agreed that if we should decline the Captain's invitation now, we might never have such a good chance again.

Yang was chosen to take up the matter with our host. "Suppose we go over together and take a look at Aquino's new hideout," Yang said cautiously to Mang Juan to broach the subject.

To our great relief the old man nodded and mildly replied, "There is no harm in doing that if you people wish to. I will go with you."

Taking advantage of a cloudy night which would help hide our identity, we left Mang Juan's place. Hiking to the Aquino's new camp was just as difficult for us as tramping to Mang Juan's had been. I supported myself with staffs hewn from sturdy branches.

"Thy rod and thy staff they comfort me."

# CHAPTER FIVE

## CAMP HOPE

*The distance traveled reveals
the strength of the horse; the
course of events tests the heart of
man.*

Chinese Adage

The solidarity of the Filipinos and the Chinese in the Philippines was borne out by the trials of the war as they joined hands and fought shoulder to shoulder as one, save for a few collaborators in both their midsts. The family tradition of both peoples and their loyalty to their friends are characteristics common to them. In my case, our Filipino friends took me, my wife and family in as their own brother and sister and close relatives without reservations.

At midnight, we reached Mt. Osboy. The Captain, with the help of the lieutenant and Rebecca, had moved piece by piece to the new spot—a nipa hut, which we called Camp I, into which his family and relatives squeezed. The Captain greeted us warmly. We all squatted on the ground outside the hut.

"Mr. Go, I know you are a man of conviction. We are of one mind. We must remain steadfast in our fight for freedom," the Captain said. "I come from Chinese antecedents, like you, and I want you to cast away whatever doubts you have about me. You can take my word that from this day on, we shall struggle together and live together, and if need be, die together." The Captain spoke from his heart. I held his hand firmly. Yang and Tony smiled with relief. Seeing that we had made up our minds to stay with Aquino, Mang Juan stood up.

23

"I shall leave you to my compadre," he said. "I am going home now, but I will try to see you again from time to time." We all thanked him for his understanding and watched him depart under the moon, which now began to shine.

The new hideout was in the heart of the jungle at the foot of Mt. Osboy. Except for an obscure trail farther north leading down to the highway, there was no path to our place. Without outsiders to annoy us, we had time for meditation. Now and then we climbed to the hilltop to view the tower of the City Hall of Manila in the distance—just to ease our longing.

I named our new home Camp Hope—hope that President Roosevelt's promised powerful help would come soon; hope that justice would triumph and victory would be ours; hope that by the grace of God, all of us in the camp and our families would survive the war without having to yield to the enemy.

Spiritually, we felt much better. Physically, there was not much improvement over the time when we were at Mang Juan's. Captain Aquino, whom we called "Aqui," was a man born for hardship. He could get by with the barest essentials, and he expected us to be as tough and thrifty as he. To survive, we had to adjust ourselves to the hardships of the wilderness.

Aqui moved all his livestock to Camp Hope. Using flattened kerosene cans taken from his old chicken coop by the roadside, he put up a flimsy 6- by 5-foot hut. It had a raised section, which we called Camp II, for Tony, Yang, and me to live in. We could not stand up straight inside the hut. We slept with the moonlight peeping in from all sides. The chickens and turkeys took refuge on the roof. Under our hut the pig grunted contentedly. Deep in the night our dreams were disturbed by the fowl's answers to the call of nature, while our entire dwelling shook each time the pig turned in his sleep or scratched his back on a post. At times, we were startled from our slumber, sure that bombs were shaking our hovel.

In the jungle, spring water was rare. During our stay at Mang Juan's we had drunk from the creek where carabao wallowed. Unused to this water, we developed stomach trouble which continued to bother us in Camp Hope. Roaming around the camp one day, Tony and Yang discovered a spring. We dug a well immediately and gloried in its clear, pure water. I remembered that Su Tung Pu, the famous Sung Dynasty scholar, rejoicing in the coming of the long-awaited rain, had sung:

> If heaven should send us pearls, none could use them
> for clothing, if heaven should send us jade, none could
> eat it as rice.

The spring discovered by Tony and Yang supplied our needs more than jewels could have done. We took it as a sign that Camp Hope was the chosen place for us.

> For he that hath mercy on them shall lead them,
> even by the springs of water shall he guide them.
> Isaiah 49:10

Though the world was in turmoil, we were grateful that among our hills we could still have the blessing of radiant days. On Sundays we gathered under a giant tree to worship God. That was our church!

Mang Juan had been indifferent when he left us. But after a few visits, he was touched by the brotherly spirit in Camp Hope. He often stayed with us overnight and joined us voluntarily in prayer. He even offered to make a trip to Manila to contact Mrs. Stagg for us.

Once in the city, Mang Juan succeeded in meeting not only Mrs. Stagg, but also my family and Yang's in the dormitory of the Cosmopolitan Student Church, which had become a refugee camp. During the early days of the occupation, American priests, pastors, and missionaries were allowed by the Japanese Army to stay within their respective compounds to look after refugees.

Immediately after our departure, Manila was buzzing with rumors. My wife took our five children and the amah, together with her brother Amado and sister Ruth, to the church dormitory for sanctuary. My mother preferred to stay behind to look after our Quezon City house at the eastern suburb of Manila. The indomitable old lady believed she could face the enemy.

When my family arrived at the church, the dormitory was already packed with other church members and their families, including Eva and Arthur. Mrs. Stagg was kind enough to share her own room with my wife and our five little children.

Many students who had come from China, Java, Singapore, Hawaii, and various provinces in the Philippines joined the refugees at the church. The crowded dormitory lacked supplies and food. My wife offered her savings to help. The younger members of the church volunteered to take care of our little ones. They all did their part to hide the identity of my family and called my wife "big sister," and Mrs. Stagg "mother." The good lady pastor was a mother to everybody. Under her devoted and courageous leadership, the entire heterogeneous group lived through the frightful days with relative calmness and with rare understanding toward each other.

On January 2, after my family had been at the church for two days, the zero hour came. The enemy marched into Manila, with General Masaharu Homma at the head. Almost all doors and windows were closed, as were those of the church, and behind them lurked the dread that Japanese soldiers might knock at any time.

On the eve of his triumphant entry into Manila, Homma sent an open letter to President Manuel L. Quezon inviting the latter to align himself with the Japanese, who according to him came as friends and as liberators of the Filipinos from the American yoke of oppression. Homma himself was a poet. Immediately, he instituted a policy of attraction aimed at winning the sympathy of the Filipino people.

A few days later, two Japanese army officers inspected the church. They came during a prayer service when everybody was at the church hall. Since the officers preferred not to interrupt religious worship, the identity of both my family and the Yangs was not discovered. Before leaving, they posted a notice at the gate instructing other Japanese armed personnel not to disturb the church. A blessed breathing spell for my family and all the others!

Except for priests, pastors, and other missionaries, American and British nationals were rounded up for concentration. Peaceful and respected families, through no fault of their own, were imprisoned in the internment camp at Santo Tomas University. Some American and British residents who escaped custody during the first few days or who remained strictly within doors were left unmolested for some time. Many, however, who visited their offices or went downtown to get news or to do necessary errands were promptly arrested.

It was among these unfortunates that the greatest distress prevailed, for they had no clothes except what they were wearing at the time. Stopped suddenly by a soldier, at the point of a bayonet, they were marched away under guard to some point of concentration and forced to stand up for several hours, sometimes in the blazing sun, waiting for others to arrive or for some Japanese officer to order them away. No food or drink was given them, no account of their physical condition was taken. Men and women were treated alike, and great suffering resulted. Usually such prisoners were told not to talk to one another, and if the sentry detected anyone breaking this command, he would at once slap the offender violently in the face. Sometimes three or four blows were given with the full strength of the arm.

General Homma dealt severely with the Americans and the British but still refrained from putting the Chinese in camps even though China was at war with Japan. He had hoped to induce the Philippine Chinese to his side.

Numbering over several hundred thousand all over the Philippine archipelago, the Chinese were mostly engaged in wholesale and retail business, supplying the daily needs of the public. To intern all the Chinese would cripple the country's economy and put a greater burden on the occupation authorities.

The first act of the Japanese military authorities against the Philippine Chinese was to confine Consul-General Kuangson

Young, his Vice-Consul K.Y. Mok and his staff, and a group of Chinese leaders at Villamor Hall of the University of the Philippines.

Vice-Consul Mok was my English editorial writer for the *Fookien Times* daily English edition. It was then the lowest priced English paper with the biggest sales. It started during the period of the Japanese invasion of Shanghai, China. The *Fookien Times* English edition, sold for one centavo per copy, was received enthusiastically by the people. It played quite an important role in building up sentiments against Japanese military aggression. During the wee hours of the morning, after we had put the paper to bed, Mok and I would go to a coffee shop and ask for strong coffee to refresh our minds. We would then discuss the topics of the day and exchange views, taking down notes for the following day's editorial.

Of the Chinese leaders confined at the Villamor Hall, naturally many were my closest friends in the anti-Japanese aggression campaign. A list of wanted men was issued. And my name was among those at the top.

My wife and our little children prayed day and night for my safety. They really did not know of my whereabouts, neither could they be sure that I was alive. The surprise visit of Mang Juan to the church was a godsend. "Thanks be to the Lord! My husband is alive," my wife exclaimed when Mother Stagg introduced Mang Juan to her. Eva, too, was overjoyed to know that Yang was well.

Upon hearing that we were living with the Aquinos, Mother Stagg decided to send two brave and trustworthy young church members, Dominador and Luis. They came to the hill with Mang Juan.

"Mother Stagg has consulted church officers on your case. Some believe you should keep away; others think you should reconsider your stand," Dominador said when he reached Camp Hope. "Every day some Chinese leaders present themselves to the Japanese Army."

This was not surprising to me. Many had no alternative and

others must have thought that the less defiance to the enemy, the better their chance for life.

"What did my wife say?" I asked.

"She didn't say what you should do," replied Dominador. "She only asked me to tell you that the children are all well in the church and that you need not worry about them."

Dominador Amor, a pleasant-looking young man, alert and determined, spoke only the words he was instructed to say with little comment on his part and he was quite unemotional. Certainly, Mother Stagg could not have chosen a better man for this mission. Later on, Dominador was to become active in the diplomatic service. After the Philippine independence, he joined the foreign affairs service; he is now the Consul General for the Philippines in Seattle.

We sent the two emissaries off the next morning with instructions to tell Mother Stagg and our families that we were fine and would keep on staying in the hills.

Six nights later Dominador burst into Camp Hope through the darkness. His face was tense. "The Japanese have seized and confiscated the *Fookien Times* and all its property," he told me. "They were furious at your refusal to surrender," he continued. "We were told the Japanese have secured pictures of you and sent them to the provinces to track you down. You might be shot on sight. Mother Stagg has asked you to grow a beard, disguise yourself and go even deeper into the jungle."

"What news do you have for me and Yang?" Tony asked Dominador.

"Bad news for Mr. Go. Good news for you two," he answered. "During the investigation your names were not mentioned by the Japanese. All your families are fine," Dominador concluded. Tony nodded. Yang kept silent.

I was like a fish in a bamboo trap. What chance has a newspaperman to beat the manhunt of the powerful Imperial Army? I thought of my friends around me; they would be involved if the enemy found them with me. Since their names were not mentioned on the wanted list, Yang and Tony could return to the city if they wished. And I could not endanger the Aquinos with their four generations—from Impo down to the baby Ophelia.

I told Tony and Yang they need not risk their lives out of pity for me. They were at liberty to seek their own way out individually.

Tony shook his head. "We decided to escape from the enemy and live a hunted life as one, and there is no reason why we should not stick together to the end," Yang said. "The report is bad for you, but who can guarantee that the events to follow will not bring us the same danger?"

The argument sounded sensible but I was in no position to comment. I left Tony and Yang and went to tell the Aquinos of Dominador's report and of the grave consequences of hiding a person so hated by the enemy.

"You are carrying the safety of four generations on your shoulders. I cannot allow you to endanger them all on my account." I hated to say it, but I had to. I wanted to relieve Aqui of his promise.

Without hesitation, the Captain held my hand. "You are to stay with us under all circumstances," he said. Aqui's indomitable spirit touched me so deeply that I could only grip his hand more firmly. The night was dark. The whole camp gathered in prayer. Many cried aloud.

Early next morning, Dominador left again. I went into the jungle. I felt miserable and terribly lonely.

> To accept death with courage at an impassioned moment is easy; To choose death after a long deliberation is difficult.
>
> Chinese Adage

This old Chinese poem expressed my mental anguish. The voice of Dominador telling me the enemy would shoot me on sight kept ringing in my ears as I plunged deeper and deeper into the jungle. Fallen trees lay here and there. Leaves fluttered to the ground as the wind blew. It was chilly.

I had conceded that the world was lost to me and that my life was forfeit to the aggressors whom I had opposed. Looking at the blue sky, I remembered how Mother Stagg had tried to console me a few months before when our sixth child, Felisa Martha, died in infancy. "Henceforth your relationship with heaven will be closer, for someone you love is there with our Heavenly Father," Mother Stagg had said.

"Does this mean the end? Am I to join my beloved baby yonder?" I asked myself.

> When a man is about to die,
>    his words are good;
> When a bird is about to die,
>    its notes are sad.

Chinese Adage

The threat of death possessed me no matter how deep into the jungle I went. "After the enemy had killed me what would happen to my helpless mother and my wife and our five children, who were mere tots and infants?" I was in great agony. My tears fell. I knelt down in the dark jungle and prayed. "Oh, Heavenly Father! Let me live!" I kept importuning. I could not depend on myself, nor could I depend on the world. I was knocking ceaselessly at Heaven's gate, for the Bible had said, "Ask, and it will be given you; seek, and you will find; knock, and it will be opened to you." I knew it was our Heavenly Father alone on whom I could depend. Leaves fell on my head as I bowed in prayer. Remembering the Bible I had brought with me, I opened it for help. As if for the first time in my life, I came across Psalm 27:

> The Lord is my light and my
>    salvation; whom shall I fear?
> The Lord is the strength of my
>    life; of whom shall I be afraid?

It gave me the courage I so badly needed. I read on:

> Though an host should encamp against
>   me, my heart shall not fear;
> Though war should rise against me,
>   in this will I be confident.

Reading this again and again, I felt a thrill I had never experienced before. I knew at that very moment that I had come face to face with the Divine Power. It was noontime. The sun's bright rays streamed straight down through the trees. I praised God for His words of deliverance and thanked Him for the strength which now sustained me. I rose with good cheer.

# CHAPTER SIX

✦❧❀❧✦

## LIKE MOTHS FLYING INTO THE FIRE

> *As the mountains are round about*
> *Jerusalem, So the Lord is round*
> *about his people.*
>
> Psalm 125:2

The tranquility was broken by the clapping of hands, Camp Hope's call for lunch; to avoid shouting names we had used clapping as a signal. I had been among the logs and the falling leaves the whole morning. In response to the call, I ran to join Tony, Yang, and the Aquinos. They were surprised to see me in fine spirits.

"Where have you been the whole morning?" Tony asked.

"I went into the jungle to appeal to God for my life and He has strengthened my heart." I explained to them what I read in Psalm 27. "I stepped into the dark jungle a lost man. My world had crumbled. Now, I am positive; I can face the situation with courage," I added. They were all silent for a while. Whether they shared my belief or not, I had no way of knowing for sure. However, it was evident that they all felt relieved that I didn't look desperate anymore.

We resumed our activities in the camp, clearing more space and exploring more secluded spots where Tony, Yang, and I could spend the days. The lieutenant who had come with Aqui left us after we had settled down.

Great was our excitement one morning when Aqui brought to camp two American Army officers, Lieutenant Spencer from New York and Sergeant Anderson from New Mexico. The whole camp welcomed them with open arms.

At first we thought the expected American reinforcements had reached the Philippines. Then we learned that Spencer and Anderson had lost contact with the main USAFFE force which had retreated to Bataan. There was very little possibility for them to cross the line. They planned to travel to the mountains north of our hideout, hoping to find other members of their unit.

"Each time we hear the zooming sound from far-off Bataan, we know the enemy is pounding our comrades," said Lieutenant Spencer. "Because of that, we can face whatever dangers may come our way."

That night the two officers cast aside all thoughts about their dangerous predicament and played gaily with the children. They joined us in our devotion. The following morning Camp Hope gave them a warm send-off. Aqui sacrificed the turkey eggs which were being hatched in the nest. Tony, Yang, and I brought out our long-hoarded Jacob's Cream Crackers. Mang Juan went to the village and brought back fresh milk. The two officers enjoyed a hearty breakfast not usual in the jungle.

We discussed the war at the breakfast table. Spencer, the young lieutenant, expressed confidence in General MacArthur's ability to hold his position in northern Australia. "Do you mean that the powerful help which President Roosevelt promised us by Christmas can only reach that far?" I asked the lieutenant.

To Lieutenant Spencer that was the best to be hoped for at that time. But we, who were still optimistic, refused to agree with him. "I do hope you are right in believing that help will come to the Philippines soon," Spencer concluded.

For a while everybody remained silent.

"We are fighting for the same cause and will have the same fate. Your danger is our danger; your victory will be our victory," I told the two American officers as they were bidding us good-bye. And I added, "Last night you had shelter; tonight you do not know where you will be. May God bless you till we meet again."

We did meet again. After two weeks Anderson returned, not with Lieutenant Spencer but with a captain named Frank.

They brought no news of reinforcements. Instead Frank said that many more American soldiers were roaming the hills. Frank and Anderson spent a morning with us, then said farewell and pushed on to the far north.

The plight of these American soldiers, drifting over a wide, lost battlefield, facing hunger, sickness, and momentary death, reminded me of these sad lines penned by an ancient Chinese poet:

> *Pitiful are the bones floating*
> *along the river of the waving tides;*
> *They remain in the longing dreams*
> *of the dear hearts at home.*

This verse describes the sacrifice of fighting men who died on the battlefields long, long ago during the Tang Dynasty (618-906 A.D.), more than a thousand years before 1942. Since then, many a war has taken place. The time may be different, the cause may be different—but soldiers die and suffer in much the same way.

The Filipino soldiers suffered, too. Upon MacArthur's order for disbandment, many Filipino soldiers had returned to their towns. But those who were from the southern island could not get home. Some were lucky enough to find shelter; others begged from house to house, getting more desperate each day. And still others, forced by hunger, took to the hills and joined gangs of marauders. Thievery became rampant. Carabaos and cows were stolen from farmers, and wealthy persons were killed. Strangers taking refuge in remote hilly regions were either blackmailed or kidnapped.

We ourselves were in danger of becoming their victims. Aqui sent for his nephew—a disbanded, stout, young soldier named Ruben Garcia—and told him to serve as our bodyguard. Every night the Captain had his gun cocked, and Tony, Yang, and I slept with bolos under our pillows. Had we been surprised by bandits, our chances would have been nil.

One night Mang Juan came to us, breathless from running,

and whispered something to Aqui. The Captain's face became grave, but he maintained his usual quiet composure. He did not disclose what he had heard. We managed to find out later that Mang Juan had encountered a member of a gang who had hinted to him that they knew of our presence in Camp Hope and suspected that we had money.

Actually, a friend of the Aquinos, who was a staff member of a bank before the war, had entrusted some of his belongings to the Aquinos for safekeeping. Although Mrs. Aquino did not know the contents, she faithfully transported the bundles from place to place. Many thought that the bundles were ours.

At high noon the next day Aqui, armed with his guns, left Camp Hope with Mang Juan. They returned in the afternoon, smiling. The Captain and Mang Juan had found the disbanded soldiers and learned that, though forced to rob for their subsistence, they still had high morale and a strong desire to fight Japanese aggression. They respected Aqui and, when told that we held the same convictions as they did, promised they would not bother Camp Hope.

In the early weeks of the Japanese invasion, not only were these disbanded soldiers eager to fight the enemy, but the bulk of the populace was expecting General MacArthur momentarily to start his counterattack from Bataan. Rumors flew thick and fast. On January 26, 1942 Mang Juan ran panting to Camp Hope and said that Manila was in total blackout. It was MacArthur's birthday. Possibly a counteroffensive was on. We all ran to the top of Mt. Osboy to see the city for ourselves. It was completely dark.

We were excited and slept little that night. But the eagerly awaited dawn brought no change. The American counterattack had not begun. Day by day the enemy reported on their advance to Bataan Peninsula. Our hopes of an early return to the city dwindled.

Dominador came once a week. He told us that during the night of the blackout the people in Manila were as excited as we were. The tension in the dormitory mounted. Valiant Mother Stagg had ordered sand to be stored in every room and told the inmates to throw sand at any Japanese who might try to enter the church premises when the fight for Manila began. But this piece of strategy was not tested.

"Most of the business houses now have reopened their doors. After all, they've got to face reality," said Dominador. Chinese traders were allowed to do business as usual. Tony's firm remained closed, pending his return. Naturally this caused Tony to worry all the more. The padlocked doors on his firm might provoke the enemy's ire.

On the 37th day of our life in the jungle, Tony left us. Through Dominador he had communicated with a lady doctor, a member of his family. The doctor had secured a pass and had come to the highway below the hills of Camp Hope with her car to take him back to Manila.

Tony explained that he had merely requested Dominador to consult the doctor regarding his situation. He had not expected the doctor to come to escort him home. We advised Tony to go with her, although we would miss him very much, having had his company to sustain us for 37 anxious days.

"You should not worry about me," Tony said with tears in his eyes as he bade us good-bye. "And if anything should happen to me in the city, you can be sure I will not squeal on you under any circumstances. Our days on this hill will stay in my memory forever."

We walked with him along the secret trail of Mt. Osboy and watched until his shadow was lost in the jungle below. After Tony's departure, the days seemed longer and harder.

A week later Dominador brought news of the imminent fall of Singapore. He had brought with him heart-shaped valentine cakes baked by my wife and Yang's. Flour was scarce at the time. Living in fear and worry, they had busied themselves the whole night. But we did not even notice that they were valentines. Worry over the bad turn of the war so occupied us that we just handed out the cakes to our companions without tasting them ourselves.

"Your wife will soon bear a child. Mother Stagg said she might need you," Dominador told Yang.

"How is Eva?" asked Yang.

"She is in fine spirits," said Dominador.

"In that case, I need not return," Yang quickly replied. But I could see the wistful expression on his face.

"Do not hesitate on my account," I said. "I will try to get along with the Aquinos' help."

For a while he was silent, then his face cleared.

"No, I have made up my mind. I will stick with you," he concluded.

After the fall of Singapore, the Japanese boasted that before long Nipponese forces would be holding a military parade in New York! We, who at first had counted the hours and then the days, realized now that it would be months, or even years, before American help could come. Not only was Eva's longing for Yang to return understandable; I, too, felt that being away from the family for an unforetold period would be impractical and unbearable. Within me there was a constant urge to go back to my family. But the search for me was centered in the Manila area. To return would be like walking into a trap, and even to think of doing so was fantastic.

Every morning after breakfast, Yang and I would go to the hilltop wooded with old trees and wild orchids where we would read the Bible and our daily devotional literature—*The Upper Room* and the *Streams in the Desert*. At noon, we would kneel together upon the rock and pour out our hearts' desires before God. Day after day we prayed to God to enable us to return to Manila to be united with our families.

There were times when we would lie on the grass, looking up at the blue sky. Like the drifting clouds, our fond hope of returning home would come and disappear. It was the middle of February. Powerfully and suddenly the sermon of the famous preacher A. B. Simpson struck me: "So long as you are waiting for a thing, hoping for it, looking for it, you are not believing. It may be hope, it may be earnest desire, but it is not faith." Simpson went further: "When ye pray, believe that ye received the things that ye desire and ye shall have them"—an extraordinary emphasis in faith which punched deep into my mind.

38

Simpson then asked: "Have ye come to that moment? Have ye met God in His everlasting now?"

I was like a dreamer who had been unexpectedly awakened by these questions.

I immediately drew the answer from another article within the pages of *Streams in the Desert,* entitled "Life of Praise." It says, "Naturally, we want some evidence that our petition is granted before we believe, but when we work by faith we need no other evidence than God's Word. God has spoken: according to our faith it should be done unto us. We should see because we have believed and this faith sustains us in the most trying places when everything around us seems to contradict God's Word." I was so inspired and actually felt that this passage was written for me.

Conclusively and in no uncertain terms, this amazing passage in "Life of Praise" declared: "We should laugh at impossibilities, we should watch with delight to see how God is going to open the path through the Red Sea, when there is no human way out of our difficulty."

From one point of view, to step out of the jungle alone would mean great danger. An even greater danger would be to return to Manila! The situation I was in was certainly as impossible as that of the Israelites facing the Red Sea. There was no safe path visible at all. But Moses in his time was willing to step on dangerous waters in faith. Since faith is the substance of things hoped for, the evidence of things not seen, I must put myself in readiness for my prayers to achieve their full impact in meeting God's everlasting now. Thus by faith, I, too, should laugh at impossibilities and see how God could open the way for me to return to my family. Meditating on this thought, I prayed for a specific promise as a go signal. My hands were guided to open *The Upper Room,* and these Bible verses appeared:

> I will deliver thee in that day, saith the Lord, and thou shalt not be given into the hand of the men of whom thou art afraid. For I will surely deliver thee,

and thou shalt not fall by the sword, but thy life shall
be for a prey unto thee because thou hast put thy
trust in me, saith the Lord.

Jeremiah 39:17-18

In the Book of Jeremiah, the weeping prophet, passages of
blessing are very rare. I was certain that God, in these wonderful verses, gave me positive assurance that I could return to
Manila to be with my family, that I need not fear for my life,
that all I required was to trust in Him. I did not have the slightest doubt that I should act right away.

> *Passive faith accepts the word as*
> *true—But never moves.*
> *Active faith begins the work to do,*
> *And thereby proves.*

Selected

"We are going home," I told Yang as I stood up. Yang was
surprised. We walked down the hill to join the Aquinos for
supper, and I told them my decision. At first they thought I
was joking.

"My whole family has witnessed your life in faith," said
Aqui. "Since you are guided to return to the city, we will go
with you."

Aqui suggested that his son, Serafin, Jr., and I disguise ourselves as sick farmers being rushed to the city for hospitaliza-
tion. He himself and Yang would ride with us. We decided to ask
the lady doctor in Tony's family to use the same car in which
she had fetched Tony and to come to Ipo to help us return. Aqui
would get a truck to take his family from Ipo to the city afterward.

Dominador came the next day to give us the latest report.
He looked graver than ever.

"The situation has turned from bad to worse," he began.
"More Chinese leaders have been forced to surrender, and
Mother Stagg has received further information which makes

40

her sure the enemy will send soldiers out to hunt for you in the hills."

This time the bad report failed to disturb me or any of the others in Camp Hope.

"We are ready to leave Ipo for Manila as soon as transportation can be arranged," I told the bewildered youth and asked him to tell Mother Stagg and my wife that God's guidance was clear and that regardless of the tense situation we would not waver.

> . . . in which it was impossible for God to lie, we might have a strong consolation, who have fled for refuge to lay hold upon the hope set before us.
>
> Hebrews 6:13

When Dominador got back to the church with the report that we were returning to the city, at first Mother Stagg was astounded. But after Dominador had carefully explained to them how I had been guided and how all of us in Ipo were determined to take the step, she offered no opposition. My wife with quiet confidence contacted the lady doctor on the telephone. The doctor came to visit her at the church and agreed to risk the trip for us.

All was set.

On the eve of our departure from Ipo, Yang and I fasted for the first time in our lives. Physically weakened but spiritually stronger, we paid a last visit to the hilltop where we had prayed together. The sun was setting, and a rainbow arched in brilliant splendor while the golden rays lit up the fields below. There was absolute silence. The power of the Creator seemed everywhere.

> As the mountains are round about Jerusalem,
> So the Lord is round about his people.
>
> Psalm 125:2

We bade farewell to Mang Juan and left the hills of Ipo on

the morning of March 2, 1942. The whole group hiked down to the same road we had traveled on the last day of 1941. True to the plan, the lady doctor and Dominador were waiting for us in the car.

As we drew closer and closer to Manila and the Japanese sentry lines, we were like moths flying into the fire.

# CHAPTER SEVEN

❧❦❧

## A WEIRD DREAM

*There is no fear in love; but per-
fect love casteth out fear.*

I John 4:18

Events were like a weird dream.

From the rocky road of Ipo to the central plain of Luzon the
villages seemed deserted, for the people avoided all unneces-
sary activity..The only sound we heard was the distant roar of
guns over Bataan Peninsula. Farther south, in Rizal Province, a
few more cars were moving. Thus more caution was required.
As we crossed Rizal on our way to northern Manila, the lady
doctor told us that Tony kept inside the house most of the time,
fearing that anything might happen. When we were approaching the boundary lines, she whispered to me, "I have little fear
of the Japanese sentries. But I am concerned over the Chinese
and Formosan spies who are collaborating with the Japanese.
They might be active around bus stations and railroad crossings,
hunting for you." She paused and then added, "I have heard
rumors which I have no way of verifying. You probably can
throw some light on them."

"What rumors?" I asked.

"It is said that the Japanese authorities have obtained con-
fidential information pointing to you as the leader of a secret
group that forced people to join the anti-Japanese boycott
campaigns before the occupation. Several other names have
been involved, too," she replied. I was silent. The good woman

discreetly refrained from following up this line of conversation.

The Japanese *Kempetai* (military police) must have succeeded in obtaining confessions from some of the Chinese leaders who were confined or imprisoned in camps. It was also possible that they gathered information from some Chinese business circle, particularly those who had become Japanese collaborators and were trading with the Japanese during the boycott movement. They must have pointed their accusing fingers at me and condemned me to the Japanese military authorities. Knowing the dangerous situation surrounding me, the lady doctor still willingly risked the trip. Our car moved on. I was deadly silent. As we drove along the highway, we felt we were stepping on thin ice atop the ocean. As the old Chinese saying goes, "Any step could cause us to drown."

As we were about to pass the sentry at the Balintawak monument—a memorial dedicated to the memory of Andres Bonifacio, the Filipino hero who had cried out for justice and touched off the Philippine Revolution—a Japanese guard approached our car.

"Where do you come from?" the guard asked.

"I am bringing an emergency patient to a hospital in Manila," the doctor replied calmly. The guard looked at the plate number of the car, then glanced at us two "sick" persons inside it. He nodded and allowed us to enter the city. We took a deep breath.

Dominador directed the driver to park at a place near the North Cemetery, just inside the city limits, and told Yang and me to alight. He refused to tell the doctor and Aqui where he intended to take us. The way Dominador acted was certainly dramatic and puzzling.

"I am sorry things have to be done this way, but I am only complying with instruction from Mother Stagg," he said.

Mother Stagg must have thought that the less the Aquinos and the doctor knew of our whereabouts, the less they would be involved. And with the least possible number of persons knowing where we were, our chances would be better.

This action, of course, amazed the doctor and the Aquinos.

Yang and I were caught by surprise, too. We had planned to stay with the Aquinos at their residence in Paco, in south Manila. In order not to create suspicion and attract the attention of passersby, we decided not to argue with Dominador and hopped on a horse-drawn rig with him. There was no time for leave-taking with the Aquinos and the doctor.

Dominador took us to the Emmanuel Cooperative Hospital, an institution affiliated with the Cosmopolitan Student Church. The hospital, a two-story building standing among shanties, was located in north Manila, not far from the cemetery. It was managed under Dr. Hawthorne Darby, formerly with the Mary Johnston Hospital, and Miss Helen Wilk—both American women missionaries and friends of Mother Stagg. Its director was Dr. Pedro Arcilla, an experienced surgeon and a trusted member of the church.

"Go into the hospital. Someone will attend to you there," Dominador told me. Reluctantly I alighted while Yang and Dominador drove off hurriedly before I could ask for an explanation. Obviously, Mother Stagg had another plan for Yang.

I had been absent from Manila only two months, but it looked like a strange world. Frightened and bewildered, I waited at the reception room of the hospital, fearing that each person who entered might be a Formosan or Chinese spy. A tall, hand-some American lady suddenly appeared. She was Miss Helen Wilk.

"Oh, you are here! Come with me," she said and guided me to the isolation room. "This is an emergency case. No one is allowed to see the patient," she instructed the nurse. Indeed it was an emergency case! Her instructions were the exact medicine I needed.

Miss Wilk had been expecting me the whole morning. The hospital and the church were working in perfect collaboration to help us. "The situation is tense and most dangerous for you," she said. "You should not expect to meet your wife. Mother Stagg will try to see you and explain the situation." She left, closing the door behind her.

The isolation room on the ground floor was about 9 feet wide and 12 feet long, like a big cage. There was a lamp, a table, a chair, and a bed. In the mountains I had had the company of Yang and the large, good-hearted Aquino family. That night, all alone, far from the hills, surrounded by four blank walls, I wondered how long I could endure. "Since God has enabled me to cross the boundary line to Manila and escape the swarming spies, He surely will not let me down," I said to myself.

I fell asleep only to be awakened by barking dogs. Peeping through the window, I felt the terror all about. Darkness covered the city.

Beginning my morning devotion at four o'clock, I read these powerful Bible verses in an old issue of *The Upper Room:*

> A great and strong wind rent the mountains and break in pieces the rocks before the Lord, but the Lord was not in the wind, and after the wind an earthquake, but the Lord was not in the earthquake; and after the earthquake a fire, but the Lord was not in the fire, and after the fire a still small voice.
>
> I Kings 19:11, 12

At that moment someone knocked at my door. It was Miss Wilk. "We are about to begin our early-morning prayer meeting, and we will sing the hymn 'Have Thine Own Way, Lord.' You are invited to join us." She handed me a hymn book and closed the door behind her.

I opened the book:

> *Have Thine own way, Lord!*
> *Have Thine own way!*
> *Thou art the Potter;*
> *I am the clay.*
> *Mould me and make me*
> *After Thy will,*
> *While I am waiting,*
> *Yielded and still.*
>
> Adelaide A. Pollard

Separated from the others by the walls of the isolation room, I joined Miss Wilk and the doctors in spirit, singing the hymn softly.

An hour later the dark clouds were dispelled by the morning light. The barking dogs gave way to the crowing of roosters. Birds chirped in the treetops. The long, fearful night had passed.

> My soul waited for the Lord more than they that watch
> for the morning.
>                                         Psalm 130:6

In spite of the danger that my presence brought to the hospital, Miss Wilk and Dr. Darby did their best to make me feel at home. They gave me books and handwritten copies of the forbidden news broadcast by William Winter from San Francisco. I followed closely the developments of the Java Sea Battle from my little isolation room. This battle was the hope we had held onto after the fall of Singapore. We had hoped that since the aid promised by President Roosevelt had failed to reach the Philippines in time, it would be diverted to rout the enemy in the Java Sea. But the day after, the Japanese boasted of victory and the San Francisco broadcast did not announce any counterclaim.

At times Miss Wilk would come to my room and we would analyze the war together. I gave her interpretations of the San Francisco broadcasts. This courageous missionary lady refused to enjoy her comparative safety by simply attending to the hospital; she risked her life to help people like me and to keep faith alive in the Allies by sending out copies of the San Francisco broadcasts.

One morning she told me, "I dreamed that a giant plane landed on the Manila shore and an American woman in khaki uniform stepped out. My first thought was for the safety of that American woman—how to hide her from the Japanese military authorities. Then I woke up."

How many of us had seen in fancy a giant American plane,

symbolizing a powerful American air armada come to our rescue? But at that time no one knew American women would join the Army as WAC's. Yet Miss Wilk had seen one in her dream. It could be only in dreams, for she was to give up her life before the WAC's arrived.

Though it was a danger spot, my little isolation room had quite a number of visitors. Dr. Arcilla, a very cautious man, came to me one night and offered me his home if I found the hospital uncomfortable. Dr. Hawthorne Darby stayed longer than her usual routine visit to share with me her Christian experiences. She was a chubby and cheerful lady whose faith was one of complete surrender to the Lord. She showed not the slightest fear.

"There was not a single day that we did not remember you in our prayers since the day we knew you were wanted by the Japanese Army," Dr. Darby said. These ladies, whose activities had never attracted my attention before the war, were deeply concerned over me during the desperate hour. It was love— Christian love.

> There is no fear in love; but perfect love casteth out fear.
>
> I John 4:18

I did not know what fictitious name Miss Wilk had given me in the hospital record. The nurses entered my room regularly to take my temperature. It was recorded in the chart that I had a fever—a fever that could easily be induced by quaking with fear!

Footsteps came and went outside my door the whole day. Many a time, when I heard footsteps, my heart would jump for fear that Japanese soldiers were coming to get me. I tried to occupy my mind by writing my memoirs or reading the Bible and other books. There were times when I questioned, "Did God allow me to return only to suffer such a predicament?"

I read the answer in *God's Grace,* a book Miss Wilk had loaned me: If God gave a person the right to make a sizeable withdrawal from the divine bank account and that person came out with only one dollar, it cannot be said that God did not fulfill His promise, but rather that this person's faith was small.

When Mother Stagg came to see me and told me that it was not advisable for me to see my wife, I fully realized that the situation must have become more serious. But I showed her the chapter I had read in *God's Grace* and told her, "God definitely assured me I could come back to the city and be with my family. Now I am in the city, and if I don't join my family, I will be just like the man who entered the bank and withdrew only one dollar."

Mother Stagg was silent. The following day she came with my wife to the hospital. Mother Stagg brought my wife to my room, then withdrew and closed the door. Poor Fely looked tense. Fear and constant worry had made her thinner. She was wearing dark glasses, a Filipino mestiza dress, and native wooden clogs. She had thought it best to disguise herself. She was both happy and scared. Our separation of sixty-two days had seemed like eternity.

We knelt together as we had done when we were about to part and thanked God that we had lived to see each other again. Tears ran down our faces.

"Our Quezon City home is unmolested so far and the children are all doing well at the church," my wife began. "But we are losing the war in Bataan. No American help has come. Day after day more of your friends are taken by the enemy or surrender." She went on to name our people who were already in confinement. "The Japanese are determined to find you," she whispered.

"Who gave you all this information?" I asked.

"Pastor Chua and Samuel Huang visit me occasionally," she replied. Rev. S.C. Chua, a pastor of the Chinese United Evangelical Church, located in the heart of the city's Chinese area, was in a position to know what was going on. Samuel Huang was our newspaper's cashier.

Many people had concluded that to defy the enemy would be like beating an egg on a rock. But to me, the fact that I had lived thus far and had seen my dear wife again meant that God would not forsake us. I was certainly not fearless, but nor was I hopeless.

She felt the hospital was not a good hiding place since even an isolation room is not spared the curious glances of people who pass in and out every day.

"Don't worry too much. God has His own way to save us. There must be a place where we can live together," I told her.

"Oh, not now. The present situation won't allow us to be together," she answered, "but I will consult Mother Stagg about another place for you." I wanted to talk about a thousand other things with her, but she had to hurry off with Mother Stagg for fear that they would be trailed by spies. After returning to the church, while resting after lunch, Mother Stagg suddenly jumped up from her bed and said, "Sister, I have definite guidance to have your husband transferred to the Dans home." The Danses were members of the church.

My wife came again to the hospital to confer with me. I was hesitant. I could only vaguely recall having met Tito Dans once at a church meeting. So I proposed moving to the Aquinos' first. Mother Stagg sent for Aqui, who gladly acquiesced. Thus, on the sixth day after my return to the city, I left the hospital.

Miss Wilk and Dr. Darby were disappointed when I said good-bye to them. They had thought of looking after me for a longer period, but since I had already made up my mind, they didn't resist. We promised to see each other again.

In the dusk Aqui and I rode in a *carromata*, native horse rig, to the Paco district. As the horse jogged along from the north to the south of the city, I noticed that the gaiety of Manila was gone. The streets were deserted and most of the houses barred. Vehicles moved at full speed. Tension over the fight in Bataan and terror of the occupation pervaded the city.

The Aquino family welcomed me, their fugitive friend, cordially. After Aqui and Junior had left the hills with us, the other members of the family had also returned to the city. Though their house was always crowded, they gave me a room to myself with all the windows closed. There was a table and chair for my use. In the next room pretty Rebecca and her younger sister Baby took turns playing the piano, filling their home with melodious tunes. They thoughtfully and kindly eased my agony with music. We all were not aware that the Japanese were close on my heels.

# CHAPTER EIGHT

❧ ⚬❀⚬ ❧

## THE FIRST RAID

> *Each dynasty has its own emperors and each regime has its own rulers.*
>
> Chinese Adage

Since the country was then in the hands of the Japanese Occupation Army, the situation was naturally reversed as compared to the short period when MacArthur organized his USAFFE to fight the Japanese. Pro-Japanese factors were then the active members of the government and the community.

In the name of "Greater East Asia Co-prosperity," General Homma recruited several local political figures for his Philippine Executive Commission. He also sponsored a Philippine Chinese Association, which pledged allegiance to him. Go Colay, a wealthy old Chinese importer who was popular among Japanese trading circles, was picked to head the association.

A Formosan doctor who served the Japanese Army as its liaison man with the Chinese association approached Pastor Chua and asked him to convince me of the futility of continued defiance. "We know he is right here in Manila," he said. "Ask him to surrender. The sooner all the prominent Chinese surrender, the earlier will all be released. You see, the Chinese consul-general and other Chinese leaders confined in Villamor Hall were treated well. The Japanese Army only wanted them to pledge their good faith and cooperation." The tune was sweet.

Pastor Chua maintained that he had no knowledge of my whereabouts. For two months the Japanese investigators in Villamor Hall kept asking about me.

52

Early one morning there was a knock on my door. It was Aqui. "The lady doctor from Tony's family is here to see you," he said.

I wondered how the physician knew I was now at the Aquinos'. She had news of Tony. Since spies had begun watching him, he had hidden at a friend's house. A new list of wanted men had been issued, and it was reported that Tony was to be in the next list. The doctor showed me a piece of paper with fourteen names. Besides mine, it bore many new names—several of them belonging to my close friends.

"Tony is anxious to contact you. He does not know whether he should surrender or run to the hills again," the doctor said. "I am opposed to his surrender. We thought of consulting you. I inquired about you from Mrs. Stagg but she refused to say anything. Finally, I thought of coming to the Aquinos'." She was eager to hear my answer.

I remembered that when Tony, Yang, and I were in the hills with the Aquinos, I had proposed to put up more huts in the jungle and have our families join us. Tony had opposed the plan then; perhaps he was considering it now. But times had changed and we lacked preparation.

I told the doctor I had long since committed my fate to God. "Tell Tony I will pray for him," I said. I did not attempt to discuss his proposal further.

The doctor was very understanding, and if she was disappointed, she did not show it. As she was leaving she said casually, "I forgot to tell you your good friend Guillermo Dy Buncio has been taken into custody."

"Guillermo arrested!" A pang shot through me. What could be the cause? The doctor had no further information except that it was becoming common knowledge that any person could be taken to the military stockade even without a reason.

Guillermo had been a conservative trader and had not taken any active part in the anti-Japanese movement. Could some personal enemy have denounced him, or had the Japanese military authorities found out his position on my newspaper? Guillermo was the chairman of our board of directors.

In December 1941, a few days before I took to the hills, I had told him that, being the head of the Board of Directors of the *Fookien Times,* he would be involved when the enemy occupied Manila. I asked him to escape with me. "Nowhere can safety be assured. I intend to stand pat and face whatever may come," Guillermo had answered. His home was only a few blocks away from where the Aquino house was located.

The raid on Guillermo's house was the first of its kind that the Japanese conducted in their search of me. They apparently had gotten wind that I had entered the city and thought I was hiding in the southern district with Guillermo.

Like a bolt from the blue, Japanese MP's forced their way into his house, ransacked every corner, and threw the whole household into a panic. Since Guillermo could neither produce me nor give any information concerning my whereabouts, the enemy took him instead.

Facing a battery of Japanese interrogators, Guillermo revealed nothing about me. Some of his relatives, however, were told by enemy spies that if they could locate me, he would be safe.

Guillermo's relatives, harassed and worried, finally found their way to the Cosmopolitan Student Church dormitory.

"We were told that the only way Guillermo can be released is by revealing the whereabouts of your husband," a relative sadly told my wife. The fact that I was the cause of Guillermo's arrest gave my wife a great shock. Between Scylla and Charybdis, she asked, "Will the Japanese release Guillermo if I take my husband's place?"

Love and devotion had overcome the fear of death and torture. She was willing to sacrifice herself but not me.

"We'll find out and let you know," said the relatives.

After they had gone, my wife telephoned Pastor Chua and told him of her offer. "Don't act in haste," cautioned the pastor.

The next day the pastor came to the dormitory. "There are no women in the Japanese camp. They will not release Guillermo because of you," he said. The good pastor strongly opposed her idea.

But a few days later, Guillermo's relatives returned. They thought my wife's idea might work.

"Give me a few days to pray and to make arrangements for our five little children," my wife explained. Poor children! They were already without a father. Are they to be deprived of their mother, too?

Guillermo's relatives were touched. They left without discussing the matter further. My wife, brokenhearted, started to pack. Except for telling Mother Stagg, she kept her plan to herself. She was determined not to let me know of this serious development and asked Mother Stagg to tell Mrs. Aquino, whom we called Sister Martha, to warn me against seeing her.

When I received the message from Sister Martha, I thought she wanted to prevent me from taking the risk to visit my wife in the dormitory, which was but a short distance from my present hideout. I did not know the perilous predicament my wife was in; neither did I know the raid on Guillermo had been primarily intended for me.

Early the following morning, during my devotion, these words came to me:

> Fear thou not; for I am with thee, be not dismayed;
> for I am thy God; I will strengthen thee; Yea, I will
> help thee; Yea, I will uphold thee with the right hand
> of my righteousness.
>
> Isaiah 41:10

Going over these verses, I could sense the presence of fearful and depressing events; I knew, therefore, that God had assured us again that we could depend on Him. Somehow, I believed my wife needed these words of encouragement as much as I did. I asked Aqui to go to the church and relay these words to her.

Aqui's call was to become a matter of life and death!

To his horror, he found my wife about to present herself to the Japanese. "The very minute you step into the Japanese garrison, it means doom for you and Mr. Go," he argued. "Whatever happens to you will eventually come to his knowledge. He would rather sacrifice himself than allow his wife to be sacrificed. Presenting yourself to the enemy will only make the situation worse. And it cannot in any way help Guillermo." Mother Stagg had not thought of this before and she was convinced now by Aqui's arguments. She joined him in dissuading my wife from carrying out her decision.

"But I have already promised Guillermo's relatives," my wife insisted.

"Time will take care of that," Aqui replied. "We must think out a new plan."

Aqui also thought it was not advisable for me to continue staying at his house. The reason was simple: The enemy might raid Tony's home, and the lady doctor might be grilled about me.

"We'd better move Mr. Go to another place while there is still time," said Aqui.

Mother Stagg's advice that we take refuge at the Danses' now became the best solution. But there was the danger that our three younger children, between two and four years old, might make noise at the Danses' and attract the neighbors' attention.

Since there was no time to lose, they arrived at a compromise. My wife, our two elder daughters—Betty and Cecilie—and I were to move to the Dans home in the adjoining district; our three younger children, Dorcie, Elsie, and Andrew, were to be taken to the Aquinos' for the time being.

Aqui hurried home. To keep me from worrying he told me simply that when he had met Mother Stagg and my wife at the church, it had been decided that I was to move to Tito Dans's house the next day. "Your wife and your two elder daughters will join you," Aqui said. "I will take care of your three younger children." Nothing else was mentioned.

I did not ask the reasons behind the new arrangement but acquiesced at once. I took it to be a step toward fulfilling God's promise. "One step at a time. God will find a way for the three little ones to join us later," I thought.

At four o'clock the following morning, March 14, 1942, I arose to read *The Upper Room*. There I read God's Word that as Isaac "removed from thence and dug for the third well, Rehoboth, it proved to be a fruitful place for him to live in." On returning to Manila I had dug my first well at the Emmanuel Hospital, the second at the Aquino house; now I would dig the third at the Danses'. Peace filled my heart that morning as I prayed with the Aquinos before bidding them good-bye again.

Aqui walked with me through the sleeping streets to the Dans house. When we quietly climbed the front stairs to the second floor, the Dans couple greeted us warmly. To avoid the attention of neighbors Aqui left immediately, and Tito led me to the ground floor where our family was to stay. This floor had been rented out until the bombing of Manila, when the occupants had evacuated to the province. Little furniture had been left behind.

"The windows are to be kept closed so the people next door will not know that you are living downstairs," Tito whispered to me. Hurriedly he went upstairs and brought down my breakfast.

My "Rehoboth" was a two-story wooden house located in a comparatively secluded neighborhood. Here Tito Dans lived with his wife, Rosario Arevalo, whom we called Sister Rosario, and their only daughter, two-month-old baby Rose Marie, whom we fondly called "Bachy." Sister Rosario's eighty-year-old mother and her two young nieces, Araceli and Esther Marcelino, also lived with them.

Tito was a short, stocky fellow of middle age. Before the war, he had worked in the registrar's office of the University of the Philippines. His wife, a very capable woman, had also worked at the University.

A sincere and humble person, Tito tried to make me feel at home. "I meet Sister Fely at the church very often. You have a fine family," he said. "Mother Stagg told me to escort them this afternoon from the church to our house."

I knelt down to pray as Tito was on his way to the church. It was no small excitement for me to count the hours.

With the door and windows closed, the ground floor was as dark as a dugout. The former occupants had left behind a skinny dog. Since the dog barked at every stranger, it was a wonder his attitude toward me was friendly, even sympathetic. He became my first companion in this new confinement.

Dusk had begun to fall. The dormitory of the Cosmopolitan Student Church was having its regular afternoon service. While the others were gathered in devotion, my wife sadly sent Dorcie, Elsie, and Andrew with their amah off to the Aquinos', accompanied by Sister Martha. Then, disguised again with a scarf over her head and wearing dark glasses, my wife brought Betty and Cecilie to the carromata which Tito had waiting. Her brother Amado and sister Ruth were to leave the dormitory and return to their parents.

She hated to leave the church without bidding good-bye to those good sisters and brothers who had lived with her in the small hall for two months during the never-to-be-forgotten difficult days. And with her promise to help Guillermo unfulfilled, she was all the more troubled.

Her one consolation lay in this wonderful Bible verse that had come to her during her meditation:

A door was opened in heaven.

Revelation 4:1

Only heaven—and nothing else—could open the door of the prison to let Guillermo out.

## CHAPTER NINE

## MARTYRDOM

*Remember them that are in
bonds, as bound with them; and
them which suffer adversity, as
being yourselves also in the body.*
Hebrews 13:3

Events followed rapidly. Two days after my family left the
church, a Chinese spy suddenly appeared. He insisted that I was
hiding in the church together with my family. "No, they are not
here," Mother Stagg answered him with finality. She marveled at
her own composure and the fact that my family had escaped by
a hair's breadth. She calmly showed the spy around the premises. Then she brought him before the church altar. "Should we
have a prayer together?" Mother Stagg asked him. Reluctantly,
he bowed his head. Before he left, he wrote a note in Chinese for
me. It read:

Please understand the situation well. Those who
voluntarily present themselves are interned in comfort-
able quarters in Villamor Hall. They are treated well.
The Japanese authorities guarantee safety to all who
present themselves voluntarily. Those who continue
to defy military authorities shall meet sure death. Make
your choice wisely.

To those who were seeking an opportunity to be turncoats, it
was an invitation. To those who were determined to resist, it was

an ultimatum. Although the note was left with Mother Stagg without instructions to be delivered, it was nevertheless meant to be communicated to me.

Having failed at the church, the spy tried to trace me through my mother at our Quezon City home. He grilled her for a long time, but his efforts were again futile. Poor mother, with her failing eyesight, had cried throughout the interrogation.

My in-laws were bothered by another Chinese spy. Both my wife's elder brother and her father had been asked, time and again, where I was hiding. This spy happened to be their family physician. He was a simple person with no ill feelings toward us. However, he had been involved in a certain case and arrested by the Japanese military police. During the investigation the enemy realized that he might be useful in locating me; therefore, one of the conditions for his release was that he work secretly to help in the search for me. He also found his way to our Quezon City home.

This new visit so frightened my mother that she moved away to a nearby village to live among Filipino friends. It was a wise decision, for soon afterward the Japanese occupied our home. The enemy took all our furniture and the Mercury car which we had used on the day of our boy's baptism.

Our newspaper plant had long since been confiscated. Now we had lost our house, too. I had brought woe to my mother, my wife, my children, my relatives, and my friends. Life at this stage was sad indeed. But we had great reason to rejoice. As the Red Sea had once opened, the way had been opened for me to come back from the hills in time to be instrumental in stopping my wife from walking into the enemy's trap. And I was alive and had my wife and daughters around me.

Day and night my wife prayed earnestly that God would set Guillermo free. Early one morning, two weeks later, after her prayer, she felt a sudden relief. "I believe Guillermo has been released," she told me. She asked Tito to go to the church to find out.

Tito was soon back with the good tidings. "Mother Stagg has heard that Guillermo was allowed to leave Villamor Hall." People were taken into confinement at just a snap of the fingers, but to get out was a different story. Certainly heaven had opened the door for Guillermo.

That neither Guillermo nor his relatives could produce me, despite harassment, was interpreted to mean—and rightly so—that he had no knowledge of my whereabouts. Further, the Japanese were convinced that he had taken no part in my anti-Japanese activities and that he could not be a menace to them. Had my wife presented herself to the authorities in the hope of saving him, she would have established the fact that Guillermo had intimate connections with us and he would have been under grave suspicion.

After Guillermo's release, other Chinese leaders, together with Consul-General Young, Consul Mok, and the entire Chinese consulate staff, were transferred to Fort Santiago, the Japanese military prison located at the old Walled City. They were scheduled to be courtmartialed.

The air was tense in the Chinese community. Pastor Chua rushed to see Mother Stagg at the Cosmopolitan Church. Upon finding that my family was no longer there, he inquired about our new hideout. He had news that the spies had intensified their hunt and that they were thoroughly checking every possible place for me, as the Kempetai were anxious to have me brought before the Military Court. Mother Stagg told him it would be better for his own safety not to know our whereabouts. Without Pastor Chua's knowing it, the enemy might try to trace us by dogging his footsteps.

Aware of our danger, another friend came to visit the church. He was Modesto Farolan, General Manager of the *Philippines Herald* and now Philippine Ambassador to Indonesia, who was then working for the Red Cross. He offered to take my children away, but Mother Stagg told him my family had left.

> The beloved of the Lord shall dwell in safety by Him; and the Lord shall cover him all the day long and he shall dwell between His shoulders.
>
> Deuteronomy 33:12

This was the assurance my wife received during her daily Bible reading the morning after she came to join me at the Dans. Since the Japanese liaison man guessed right that I was in Manila, and the Japanese spies were following every step of our move, and with the men wanted by the Kempetai being arrested one after the other, none would ever imagine that we could live inside the city, evade the searching eyes of the spies and escape the enemy man-hunt. "The Lord is certainly covering us every minute of the day, all the day long," my wife Fely said.

Inside our dark quarters, with the sultry summer setting in, we eagerly looked forward to nightfall. We would wait until our neighbors were asleep, and then open the small back door; we would gaze at the sky over the wall in the backyard and feel the gentle breeze touch our cheeks.

The familiar staccato calls of lizards reminded us of home. Fireflies came and went in the yard. The skinny dog took the opportunity to walk outside. "Mama, why can the dog go out and not we?" Cecilie innocently asked her mother one night. My wife kept silent.

"Poor children, we have been deprived of the liberty that even a small dog may enjoy," I sighed as I caressed Cecilie and Betty. I could not give full vent to my emotions for fear the children might lose control and cry.

My wife bit her lips for a while and then changed the subject. "Look at that group of stars. They form the same cross we used to see at home," she said tremulously.

Darkness had covered the world, but it could not touch the brightness above.

The Danses were very kind. They cooked our meals, which they lowered to us in a basket through a square hole sawed in the floor. Whenever we heard the bell ringing upstairs, it meant the basket would be lowered. Our two daughters most eagerly awaited the tinkling summons. The harder conditions became, the tastier was our rationed food.

Our two families had become close and familiar friends. Tito and Sister Rosario would sneak down quietly to join us in our nightly prayer. We poured out our hearts together. We had an

62

electric bulb which we covered with black paper. The moon and the stars gave us added light.

It was Mother Stagg who had asked Tito Dans to shelter us, and he had agreed to the dangerous proposition without hesitation. He and his wife loved the missionary as their own mother. "I will have no regrets even if I lose my life," Tito assured Mother Stagg.

Sister Rosario's opinion had always been highly respected by her husband, who never made any commitments without first consulting her. But in this particular case, he acted entirely on his own. This surprised not only his wife, but Tito himself.

"When Tito told me that he had consented to Mother Stagg's proposition, I was surprised," Sister Rosario told me. "I asked him if he knew you were among the most sought-after enemies of the Japanese. And he answered, 'Yes, I know, but if it is God's guidance that they should stay with us, who am I to stop it?' So, from that time on we prayed that if it was God's will the way would be opened, but if it was not His will all avenues would be closed. Since your arrival we have had peace in our hearts. We are now fully convinced that it is God's way of helping us grow spiritually—letting us share your life in exile."

The University of the Philippines suspended classes from the time of Pearl Harbor through the early days of the occupation. Tito, who was no opportunist, was content with selling fruits for a living. When we joined the Danses and formed a cooperative household, we combined our resources, and Tito was able to quit selling fruits and to devote his full attention to looking after us all.

At dusk, he would court danger by going to a friend's house to tune in secretly on the "Voice of Freedom," a USAFFE broadcast from Bataan conducted by Salvador P. Lopez, a brilliant newspaper colleague and a friend of mine, who served as Philippine Ambassador to London, Paris, and Washington after the war and now as President of the University of the Philippines. Through this broadcast we learned of General MacArthur's departure from Bataan. And through it also we heard MacArthur's promise, "I shall return!"

Through the little information we received we knew the aging General Jonathan Wainwright, second in command to Mac-Arthur, was desperately waging his losing fight.

The battle for Bataan reached its critical point during Holy Week, which came early in April. It was then that I had a deeper understanding of Apostle Paul's letter to the Corinthians which read:

> We are troubled on every side, yet not distressed; we are perplexed, but not in despair; persecuted, but not forsaken; cast down, but not destroyed; always bearing about in the body the dying of the Lord Jesus, that the life also of Jesus might be made manifest in our body.

Bataan fell on April 9, 1942. The remaining American and Filipino forces retreated to the Corregidor island fort, which was bombed day and night. Soon the infamous Capas Death March began. Filipino and American war prisoners—starved, exhausted, and tortured—were forced to march 49 miles from Bataan to Camp O'Donnell in Tarlac Province, lying in the heart of central Luzon. Many died on the way.

Secure in their victory, the enemy dropped their conciliatory attitude toward the non-cooperating Chinese. Consul-General Young was forced to choose between death and soliciting a huge sum of money from the Chinese nationals for the Japanese war chest. The Consul-General rejected the enemy's invitation to collaborate. Together with Consul Mok and six others of his staff, he bravely met his end—an execution in total disregard of international law.

Preceding the deaths of these eight officials came those of ten Chinese civilians—seven of them were members of the anti-Japanese boycott movement. All were forced to dig their own graves.

Over thirty Chinese leaders were sentenced to either life or long-term imprisonment and thrown into cells with whatever they were then wearing. They had to sleep on the cement floor, like hogs before the slaughter. Time and again I cried to myself as the weeping prophet Jeremiah did.

> Oh that my head were waters and mine eyes a fountain of tears that I might weep day and night for the slain of the daughter of my people!

I thought of those who died on the battlefields and on the execution ground. Death is received in different ways. As an old Chinese saying affirms, to some death is light as a feather, to others heavy as a mountain.

I recalled the martyr of the Sung Dynasty, Wen Tien-Hsiang (1236-1281 A.D.), who persistently refused to surrender and cooperate with the Mongolian conquerors. When he was about to face execution, he wrote the following conclusions:

> Such is the grand and glorious spirit which endureth for all generations, and which, linked with the sun and moon, knows neither beginning nor end. The foundation of all that is great and good in heaven and earth, it is itself born from the everlasting obligations which are due by man to man.

In the Bible we are told, "Fear not, fear not those which kill the body, but are not able to kill the soul."

The misfortune that had befallen the martyrs and the many captives could befall me at any moment. In my dreams I was with them in the graveyard and in the prison cell.

> Remember them that are in bonds, as bound with them; and them which suffer adversity, as being yourselves also in the body.
>
> Hebrews 13:3

# CHAPTER TEN

❧

## THE DAY CORREGIDOR FELL

*And we have known and believed
the love that God hath to us. God
is love; and he that dwelleth in
love dwelleth in God, and God
in him.*

I John 4:16

Notwithstanding the terror that was rampant, we observed a
very special occasion.

For many years on April 21, the Danses had celebrated
Mother Stagg's birthday, and they kept this tradition.

Cheerful and enthusiastic as usual, Tito made a wooden ladder which he lowered through the hole used for the food basket,
and we all climbed upstairs for a royal feast.

Mother Stagg arrived on time. We all greeted her joyously.

The Psalmist has said, "Thou preparest a table before me in
the presence of mine enemies." How well we understood this
now! We were feasting in the heart of an enemy-occupied area.
If a spy had followed this American lady, who was obliged to
wear a red identifying arm band which attracted much attention
when seen in the streets, our place would surely have been
raided.

We discussed the resistance movement.

"Many Filipino soldiers had the courage to run away while
marching to Camp O'Donnell," Mother Stagg eagerly told us
when the soup was served. "And some have come to me for
clothing and help. Organized resistance will begin soon." In

fact, some young soldiers were already working as messengers at Mother Stagg's church.

I knew the gallant mother deemed it her duty to join in the resistance movement and had made up her mind to defy the aggressors to the very end. But I could imagine that because of her kindheartedness and her trusting nature, she could easily fall a victim to the enemy's deceit.

"When men come to ask for your help, you must beware of the enemy's counterintelligence operators. They pose as sympathizers so as to unearth secrets," I warned her.

"No matter what happens, I am prepared!" she said. "Even if the enemy should cut me here." And she drew a line across her neck. We never expected her to make such a grim declaration on her birthday.

We read Psalm 91 to her to wish her long life. She was happy, but seemed indifferent about reaching a ripe old age. She thanked the Danses for their love and promised to come back and see us when another opportunity offered. Then she kissed all our little ones good-bye.

Quietly we climbed down the wooden ladder to our ground quarters to resume our daily routine. Our two daughters spent most of their time on the ground floor in the room at the back, cutting paper toys to while away the time. My wife read her Bible between dishwashing chores. Tito had fixed a table for me and gave me plenty of writing paper from the University of the Philippines. I worked continuously on my memoirs in the anteroom just inside the main door, which was always kept closed.

Early one afternoon the door suddenly opened. A tall young man walked in. I was caught completely by surprise. He stared at me for a moment and then withdrew.

Who could he be? What would he say about finding me living in the dark on the ground floor?

I learned later that a few hours before, Tito had come down to the ground floor and left by this front door, forgetting to lock it. Anybody could have entered our hideout any time that afternoon. The young man was a former occupant, a Reserve Officers Training Corps' (ROTC) member who had joined the army.

He was one of the prisoners who had escaped from the Death March and had come to the Dans house to get his ROTC cap which had been left there. Our encounter was a meeting of two surprised fugitives!

"The young man does not know who you are," Tito said. "I believe he won't talk," Sister Rosario added. However, my mind was troubled by that incident. After nights of prayer, the Danses thought of a new plan. They put flower pots along the windows upstairs to shut out the neighbors' view. Then they transferred us to the second floor, while the nieces and the mother of Sister Rosario moved to the ground floor and kept the front door open to give the neighbors the impression that they now occupied the whole house. They thought this would remove suspicion in case the young man should talk. This plan not only lessened our suffering from the summer heat, but was to help us when the enemy's house-to-house search started.

On the second floor were a master bedroom, a living room, a dining room, and a kitchen. Between the kitchen and the bedroom, which was occupied by the Dans couple, there was an empty storeroom. At night this storeroom and the dining room became our sleeping quarters.

The Danses stayed on the ground floor to receive visitors during the daytime. Their niece Araceli came upstairs every day to give Betty and Cecilie English lessons. Every night after dinner, Tito and Sister Rosario would join us in Bible studies in the kitchen.

The more we shared each other's experiences, the firmer our convictions became and the keener we understood each other's problems.

Many a time, as the evening church bells pealed, my wife lapsed into silence, filled with longing for Dorcie, Elsie, and Andrew, who also must have heard the bells. Though only a few blocks from the Dans house, they seemed miles away.

The sympathetic Tito offered to accompany my wife to the Aquinos' for a short visit. She ventured forth with him one night and stayed three days with our darling little ones. Poor children, so young and innocent, how they had pined for her motherly care! The day these little ones had left the church, they were entirely at a loss. Upon their arrival at the Aquinos' Dorcie had cried for hours for Mama. It took our amah, Louisa, a long time to calm her. Louisa herself did not know where my wife and our two elder daughters had gone, for Mother Stagg and Aqui thought it safer that way.

Louisa was a middle-aged Cantonese woman. She had been widowed at 18 and had been with us for four years, caring for our children. Now she had to suffer and risk her life with us in exile.

"How are the children?" I asked my wife upon her return.

"They have been crying for me and are getting thinner," she said with a heavy heart. "I do not know how long the children can continue like that."

"We have God's promise." This was the only answer I could give. "Let us trust that soon they will be united with us." And it did come to pass.

On the day Corregidor fell, Sister Rosario hurried home from church with the shocking news that the lady physician in Tony's family had been arrested. Tony's name was on the latest "wanted" list, but he had refused to surrender. The spies seized the doctor and were trying to force her to reveal his hiding place.

This became a grave emergency involving all of us. Could the doctor endure the torture? What if the enemy forced her to reveal her knowledge of Tony's connection with Aqui, Yang, and me? Aqui had thought of that once, and thus I had moved out of his house. Now when the worst had occurred, we began to think further. Should the enemy find our three little children at the Aquinos', they would not only take them as hostage, but there would be ample evidence against the Aquinos for sheltering "wanted elements." And more complications could follow. The fate of one becomes the fate of all. Under these circumstances, the Danses suggested that our three little children move immediately from the Aquinos' and join us. Since we now stayed upstairs and the neighborhood believed the Danses occupied the whole house, they might not be curious should they hear noise made by the children.

Arrangements were made accordingly.

Early on a May morning, Aqui and Sister Martha, together with our amah, brought Dorcie, Elsie, and Andrew through the misty streets to the Danses'. It was indeed a touching sight to see our three innocent little ones run to the bosom of their mother. Their separation from me had been almost half a year; I had become thinner and had grown a beard. No wonder they could hardly recognize me. Poor children, they must have thought that their daddy was gone forever. As I held them in my arms, my heart overflowed with gratitude. The reunion which God had promised while I was in Ipo had come about. We all knelt down to offer a prayer of thanksgiving.

> And we have known and believed the love that God
> hath to us. God is love; and he that dwelleth in love
> dwelleth in God, and God in him.
>
> I John 4:16

The three little ones had arrived during an interlude between storms.

The lady doctor had been tortured for days but had courageously refused to talk. Tony, who could stand it no longer, presented himself at the military camp, and the doctor was released. He was handcuffed and thrown into Bilibid Prison, where he received neither food nor water for four consecutive days. The enemy thought rough treatment would break their prisoner's morale and hasten confession, but Tony kept the pledge he had made. He never told on us. When the enemy failed to find enough evidence to warrant his death, they sentenced him to a long term in prison. He was transferred to Muntinglupa, a prison in Rizal province, about 17 miles south of Manila. .

We grieved for Tony. The day Tony, Yang, and I trod the road to self-exile, we had said we would live or die as one. But as time passed, it turned out that he was much better off separated from us. Many things lie beyond human design. Just now, Tony was suffering more than we ever dreamed he would. Every night, as I stretched out on the mat Tony had given me the day before he left Ipo, I could hardly forget him.

More persons were taken into custody after the fall of Corregidor. President Manuel Luis Quezon, accompanied by his family and Vice-President Sergio Osmeña, left the Philippines with General MacArthur for Australia and, ultimately, the United States. From his U.S. headquarters Quezon sent broadcasts to his people in the Philippines to continue the resistance. This served as a rallying point, raising the hope and morale of the beleaguered Filipinos.

The Japanese on May 6, 1942, proudly broadcasted their victory over the islands' last and strongest fortress and put General Wainwright before the microphone to order all USAFFE forces to lay down their arms and surrender.

In a Chinese broadcast that same evening the vice-president of the enemy-sponsored Philippine-Chinese Association urged the anti-Japanese Chinese in the Philippines to cease their defiance and start cooperating with the new regime. He offered the opportunity especially for these Chinese to come to their fold. He was a very close friend of my late father and very fond of me. His was an eloquent speech, but it failed to move me.

Our hopes rose above this temporary adversity of war. That very day I read in the Book of Genesis about Noah's Ark. The story tells of the flood which rose continuously for 150 days and then started to subside. I showed the passage to my wife and the Danses. "This is our hope," I pointed out. The story of Noah in the Ark was not necessarily a prophecy which might refer to the war we were in, but God could use His own Words in the Holy Book to enlighten us, to give us hope and courage, on any occasion He chose.

On the 150th day of the Pacific War, Corregidor fell. The Japanese military gains reached their peak at the same stage that the flood had risen to its height. When I drew the parallel between the war and the biblical story for my wife and the Danses, I did not have the faintest idea that the Battle of the Coral Sea was raging. Nevertheless, I clung to the belief that from that day on the enemy's war fortune would be on the decline, like the flood. Exactly 151 days after the Pacific War broke out, on May 7, 1942, Japan suffered its first setback in the Battle of the Coral Sea.

In different war theaters devout people had taken refuge in God as Noah had. Like Noah in the Ark, we kept a family of eight inside the Dans house. The Ark had been lifted closer to heaven with the rising flood. We, too, were drawn nearer to God as the danger mounted.

With the USAFFE's main strength broken in Bataan and Corregidor, the enemy now controlled the whole Philippine archipelago from Luzon to the Visayas and Mindanao. Then came the report of Supreme Court Justice Jose Abad Santos' martyrdom. When President Quezon and Vice-President Osmeña left for America, Santos had chosen to remain in the Philippines to carry on the fight. From Bataan Santos went to Cebu, where he was captured with his son by an enemy patrol in Barili. Later they were transferred to Malabang, in Lanao. This great Filipino patriot refused to cooperate with the enemy. Ordered on pain of death to find and secure the surrender of General Manuel A. Roxas, who later became President of the Philippine Republic, Santos would not budge. He was executed on May 2, 1942, defying the enemy up to the last moment of his life.

Before his execution, he told his son, Pepito, "I have been sentenced to death. They will shoot me in a few minutes." Pepito broke down and cried. "Do not cry. Show these people how brave you are. It is a rare opportunity to die for one's country. Not everybody is given that chance," he said, kneeling down to pray with his son. Then he rose and marched boldly to his death.

I had known him personally and was greatly shocked when Tito told me the sad story. I was moved to exclaim, "Jose Abad Santos is dead, but the soul of the Philippine nation lives!"

# CHAPTER ELEVEN

## THE SEARCH

> *To conquer the people's hearts is*
> *of the highest order.*
> *To conquer a city is of the lowest*
> *order.*
>
> Chinese Adage

The enemy had occupied the Philippines but so far had failed to win the people.

"There is a new broadcast!" Tito announced excitedly. "It is the 'Voice of Juan de la Cruz' and it protests against the cruelty of the enemy." The broadcast had created quite a sensation. Brave were the men who risked their lives to cry for justice!

Unfortunately the secret station was soon tracked down by the enemy and paid for with many lives.

Then, the enemy announced that anyone found harboring hostile persons would be severely punished. A search was launched in certain districts.

Aqui came to me suddenly one afternoon. This was unusual because he had always visited us under cover of night. He had resumed his former job with the Bureau of Education and had been assigned to work in Mindoro, an island province south of Manila. Now and then, he made trips to visit his family in the city.

He told me that Yang had fled to his house and had hidden there for a day. I had not heard from Yang since we separated at the Emmanuel Hospital in March, but I knew he was living opposite the hospital with Max Lazo, a former YMCA worker.

Lazo's wife, Dahlia, a nurse in the Emmanuel Hospital, had the confidence of the three American missionaries.

"Many people have been taken lately in the northern district. Peeping through holes in the shell-paned window, Yang saw how his neighbors were herded into the army truck. He was able to slip out," Aqui said. As usual, Yang had been quick-witted. "Before he returned to the Lazo's, Yang and I talked a long time about going back to the hills. I want to know what is in your mind now," Aqui added.

"I planned to take our families to live in the hills at the beginning of the occupation, but now I have stopped thinking about it," I replied. "I feel settled living here with my family." I did not realize how bluntly I spoke. Aqui cut short the generous proposal he was about to make.

"The search has started in north Manila, and it will soon reach the south side. You should be prepared for it," he warned me and left.

Aqui's prediction came true—one morning, a few weeks later, while Sister Rosario and Tito were out. Suddenly, Araceli ran upstairs, trembling. "Japanese soldiers are guarding both sides of our streets," she said breathlessly. "They are stopping people from going out and are searching from house to house."

We were caught like turtles in a big jar. There was nothing we could do! To run out would be an invitation for them to capture us.

We had lived every moment in faith. The famous preacher C. H. Spurgeon said in one of his sermons that faith was like swimming. When one thrust oneself into the water with full trust, the water would keep him afloat. Every time before I went to sleep, I would pray and say to God, "Dear Father, I put full trust in Thee as I am plunging into the water." I took my usual nap that day. It was my wife who awakened me.

"The soldiers are continuing their search and are approaching our neighborhood," she said. "They are only a house and an empty lot away from us."

Obviously they had been searching for a long time and had

still not been able to find their quarry. I kept wondering whether they were looking for us or for somebody else.

My wife and I were on our knees in prayer when Sister Rosario returned. She told us that as she was entering the door, two Japanese soldiers passed by and cast a casual glance at her. A few moments after, she said, a car ground to a sudden halt in front of the house. An officer, alighting, stood looking into the ground floor for a while, and then abruptly crossed the street. We had moved upstairs so that the door to the ground floor was not kept closed. Otherwise it would have drawn suspicion.

The search went on grimly until sunset. A Filipino woman accused of guerrilla sympathies was dragged away. The soldiers did not enter the Dans house.

> The angel of the Lord encampeth round about them
> that fear Him and delivereth them.
>
> Psalm 34:7

After our narrow escape from the enemy's search, sickness attacked us. Our daughter Betty contracted dysentery. She ran a very high fever. She kept shouting deliriously, "Fire!" I could feel the burning within her body. Keeping vigil over her as she fought for her life, my wife and I fasted in prayer.

"My little daughter," I told Betty, "God has saved us from death on many occasions. He surely is capable of curing your illness." Betty nodded. All we gave her was water.

Twenty-four hours later she was out of danger. After this experience, we were fortified to meet an even greater test. Little Elsie had convulsions. Poor Louisa thought her case was hopeless. Elsie, too, was cured.

St. James said, "The prayer of faith shall save the sick." We certainly experienced it. Tito and Sister Rosario were inspired and relayed it to the three American missionaries. The ever-cheerful Dr. Darby came to visit us.

From her I learned about the suffering of my friend Roy Bennett and his family. When Manila was occupied, Roy sat tight in his home, as he had advised me to do. Mrs. Bennett and their children were interned, but Roy had been imprisoned at Fort Santiago and thrust into a dirty cell, like my grand old friend F. Theo Rogers, General Manager of the Philippines Free Press, and other "special prisoners." These unfortunates were deprived of food and water for days.

"God has sustained Mrs. Bennett in her most trying hour and the same can be said of the other internees," Dr. Darby said before she bade us good-bye. The internees at Santo Tomas Camp had organized so as to help each other through persecution and privation. Outside the camp walls Catholic priests, Protestant missionaries, laymen, sympathizers, and friends gathered food and other supplies and sent them in to the internees.

> There is neither Jew nor Greek, there is neither bond nor free, there is neither male nor female: for ye are all one in Christ Jesus.
>
> Galatians 3:28

Not long after Dr. Darby's visit, on a cloudy September afternoon, Mother Stagg dropped in on us unexpectedly. She wore a white blouse with a black skirt. Her face was drawn. "I bring you bad news," she said. My heart sank. "Where is Sister?" she asked, referring to my wife. "Her mother died this morning."

My wife entered the room in time to hear of her great loss. Her mother had been a very kind old lady who had suffered a long illness. "In her last moments, she mentioned you all again and again," Mother Stagg said, repeating what my brother-in-law, Amado, had told her. My wife broke down. Mother Stagg wept for a while; then she remarked, "Sister, the Lord has said: 'Other sheep I have, which are not of this fold: Them also I must bring, and they shall hear my voice; and there shall be one fold and one shepherd.' " Knowing my wife was concerned for her mother's soul, the good lady pastor tried to comfort her. "Your mother lived a good life. Though she was not baptized before she passed away, the Lord has not forsaken her." Mother Stagg tenderly held my wife's hands.

It was even riskier for Mother Stagg to call on us at this time than at the time when the Danses had celebrated her birthday in April. Her activities had aroused suspicion, and the enemy garrison commander had ordered her to appear in person once a month at their headquarters to give an account of what she was doing. The garrison commander expected her to answer questions each time she was interviewed. Although under surveillance, she persisted in helping the underground. Her absence from the church at this time could possibly have been checked by the enemy. The longer she stayed away, the more risk she ran.

"I hate to leave you in a hurry but I have to," she said as she bade us farewell. "I shall keep in touch with Amado."

We could not even attend the funeral because the search for me had been intensified. Spies were seen among the mourners, on the lookout for my wife. Our participation in the funeral rites would only have led to further sorrow.

My wife cried the whole afternoon. Outside it was dark and lowering, for the rainy season had come. I had nothing to say and little comfort to offer. That night the wind lashed the houses and the rain drove down in torrents. Everyone else in the house was asleep. Alone with my thoughts, I meditated on the tragedy of death. Every hour, every moment, men and women were dying in battle, in persecution, in hunger, and in sickness. What about the souls of those who lived a good life, who fought a good fight, and who died without being baptized? Was there any hope for them? I pondered this question. It was two o'clock in the morning. My eyes lighted upon this Bible verse:

> Else what shall they do which are baptized for the dead, if the dead rise not at all? Why are they then baptized for the dead?
>
> I Corinthians 15:29

I repeated it many times, wondering at the immeasurable love of our Heavenly Father and His omniscience and omnipresence.

My wife fasted in prayer for 49 mornings in memory of her mother.

77

# CHAPTER TWELVE

✥

## DILEMMA

*Teach me thy way, O Lord, and
lead me in a plain path, because
of mine enemies.*

Psalm 27:11

With the failure of the spies to trace my whereabouts, rumors
went wild. One told of my being killed in the battle zone before
the fall of Bataan. Another claimed I was in active command of a
guerrilla unit. Still another reported that the enemy had put a
prize on my head.

We left everything to God and celebrated quietly the National
Day of the Republic of China—October 10, 1942. I asked my
wife to give the children each an egg. What a luxury! In our
tradition the roundness of the egg symbolizes unity and blessing.
We prayed for China and for the success of our allies.

This great day was followed by another—October 20, our
tenth wedding anniversary. Again, each child enjoyed the luxury
of a whole egg.

That afternoon, I continued my writing.

"I just heard Mother Stagg is on her way to see us," my wife
whispered to me. Something important must have happened or
she would not be taking such a risk, I thought. It turned out that
the Danses had invited her to attend the surprise supper they had
prepared for us!

Ten years before, Mother Stagg had assisted her husband, Dr.
Samuel Wells Stagg, in officiating at our wedding ceremony.
Now we had fled from our home and Dr. Stagg was away—his

fate unknown. Only Mother Stagg was there to reminisce about old times with us. I remembered the marriage vows:

> . . . in sickness or in health, in wealth or in poverty,
> for better or for worse, until death do us part.

War could not separate us. Suffering only brought my wife and me closer to each other. Our five children around us were sufficient reason for us to look to the future.

Betty and Cecilie had progressed much in their English lessons with Araceli. Dorcie began to show her love for music. Elsie was acting very independent in her cute little way. Andrew, the little boy who was beginning to toddle when we left home, was now taking part in the children's daily devotion and joined his sisters in reciting Psalm 128.

This beautiful Psalm gives the blessed promise that those who fear God and walk His way will live to see their children's children. We asked our little ones to memorize it in their daily afternoon devotion. My wife and I craved this promise even while we were in exile, and we looked forward to its complete fulfillment in the days to come. First, we had sought God merely for refuge, but the more we learned of His wonderful love, the more we treasured His Word and sought His blessings.

At the table Mother Stagg expressed her joy to find all our children growing so fast. Since the time they roomed with her in the early days of the occupation, they had been as dear to her as her own children.

"What do you think of the war situation now?" Mother Stagg asked me with a twinkle, referring to our conversation at Andrew's baptismal party a little over ten months before, when I had said the Japanese would not be so stupid as to involve the Philippines in war.

"The tide of war has definitely turned in our favor," I answered. In Midway Battle in the central Pacific, the fleet led by Admiral Raymond A. Spruance had forced the Japanese Navy under Admiral Yamamoto to retreat; and General MacArthur's counterattack from the southwest had succeeded at Guadalcanal and the Solomon Islands.

"Many people think it will be a long time yet before victory comes," Mother Stagg commented. She then talked about the growing guerrilla movement in the Philippines. The courageous woman was more determined than ever to carry the fight through, no matter how long it took. It was almost dusk when she left for the church.

For a short time the tension eased after General Homma was replaced by General Shigemori Kuroda. Some Filipino war prisoners were released. A few Chinese leaders with light records were also freed from prison. But this seeming laxity did not mean the enemy had given up the hunt for hostile elements. During Kuroda's time "Neighborhood Associations" were organized. These were very familiar to the Chinese, for they followed a system practiced in China long ago. A group of ten houses formed an association which was responsible for any untoward incidents occurring among its members. Each association was required to report on any suspected person within it. I would have been discovered easily if the Filipino people in our neighborhood had carried out the new project wholeheartedly.

The Kuroda regime also initiated a political training program to teach the Japanese ideology. Officials connected with public education were called for a two-month training course. Tito, who by then had resumed his work with the University of the Philippines, was obliged to enroll. I knew that no amount of indoctrination would alter Tito's firm convictions. But I had trusted that since it was God's plan that we continue our stay at the Dans house, Tito would be excluded from the training.

Tito packed up and said good-bye, regretting that he had to leave us at a time when we needed him. "I still believe you will not have to leave us. God will have His way," I told him.

A few days later, Tito rushed home from the university camp, his face flushed with excitement. "I did not have to go on with the training," he exclaimed. Tito had been selected to undergo the course along with twelve other staff members of the University. Then it was decided that one should be left out to make the group an even dozen, and Tito was spared.

Soon came Christmas 1942. Tito managed to get some toys for the children. He picked up a few dry branches, tied them together, and decorated them with colored paper to simulate a Christmas tree. Just a year before, a green Christmas tree stood deserted in the living room of our home in Quezon City, its multicolored bulbs unlit, for the city was under a blackout. In an air-raid shelter our family crouched while enemy bombers circled overhead. We hoped then that American reinforcements would come in time to save the Philippines from being occupied. Now we could only hope that the Japanese occupation might soon be over.

Having experienced oppression, one feels the joy of redemption more intensely. Daylight was about to break when my wife and I finished our morning worship. We both felt Christmas within our hearts as we had never felt it before. "I in them, Thou in me," Christ had said to our Heavenly Father. In darkness we had light. In hopelessness we had hope. The Lord had found us in a lost world and brought us into oneness with Him. It was a merry Christmas indeed.

The wonderful Yuletide was soon over. It was 1943 and another year. Many a night I carried my little girl Elsie on my shoulders. She looked through a high window, where no neighbor could see her, and gazed at the moon. "The moon is high, the sky is blue, here am I, where are you?" she sang. This sweet little voice expressed our longing for home. Being confined in a small house, walking on tiptoe, and talking in whispers made our stay at the Dans home seem like ages. We were bored at times and so were the Yangs in their new home.

The first few months after Yang's return from Ipo, he and his family had lived a contented life with the Lazos. Eva gave birth to another boy, Benny; both mother and child were well. Occasionally, Dr. Darby and Miss Wilk would cross the street from the Emmanuel Hospital and see them.

Although Yang's name was not on the enemy's wanted list,

it was understood that the enemy had hoped he would offer to collaborate. For some time they had waited for Yang to come forward and serve as secretary of the Chinese Association. But they finally had to appoint another man.

After the enemy had conducted their search on the city and its suburbs, Yang woke up to the fact that Manila was no longer a safe hiding place and wished to talk about future plans with me. Through Dr. Darby and Tito, it was arranged for us to meet at the Danses'—a simple enough meeting but a dangerous one.

On a breezy night early in January 1943, Yang and Eva arrived quietly. Our conversation filled hours. We had so much to tell each other!

"When I ran to Aqui during the search of the northern district, I proposed that we take our families to the hills as you had suggested when we were in Ipo," Yang said. "A year has passed. I believe we have to do more waiting and we should not stay in the city any longer."

For hours we analyzed the situation, comparing the merits of the city and the hills. We shuddered to think what could happen if we remained in the city and someone so much as pointed an accusing finger at our hideout or if a gust of wind carried news of us to the ears of a spy. A knock at the door and we would be goners. But if we lived in the mountains, even if the enemy should obtain information about us, it would take them time to send troops out and these could possibly get lost in the midst of so many hills with their overgrown trails. In the wilderness at least we would not feel trapped like turtles in a jar.

"Trials and temptations in the city are greater and they tend to weaken our convictions," Yang remarked. "Life in the secluded hills can be simpler as we will be left to ourselves." I could understand what was in Yang's mind. For if Yang decided to join the enemy, he could be an influential man and have the same opportunity for personal aggrandizement as other collaborators enjoyed. The simplest way to avoid temptation, of course, was to keep away from it. But to move the two families to the hills now would be more difficult than during the early days of occupation. The situation had become more complicated. One slightest mistake could prove fatal to all. We decided not to act hastily but to bring the matter before God. The Yangs left the next night.

For two months we prayed for guidance.

"Yang sent this note to you," Tito told me one day when he came home from church. In his quiet hour of meditation, Yang said in his note, the story of Caleb had come to him. During Joshua's time Caleb was sent to the hilly land for the second time and he went courageously. We had entered the Ipo hills once, and Yang believed that, like Caleb, we should enter the hills a second time.

When I took the matter up with my wife, she strongly opposed taking our family to the hills. She pointed out that Ipo was a malaria-infested area. The jungle would not be a healthy place for the children. Communication was difficult. We would encounter no end of trouble in obtaining our daily needs. "Once in the mountains, we will be isolated and at the mercy of robbers," she said. "And suspicion will be aroused among the mountain folk. How can we hide our identity?"

I could not ignore my wife's reasoning, but I also had reasons in subscribing to Yang's plan. I told her that once inside the jungle, the children would be free to run around. They would have fresh air and would no longer be denied normal childhood activities. They could talk aloud, not in whispers. We could raise chickens, pigs, cows, and vegetables. "During the days when Tony, Yang, and I were there, banditry was rampant. But conditions are different now. The mountain folk have settled down to their quiet life. They are simple and honest. In the jungle trees and bushes serve as natural hiding places. Houses are far apart. There will be no curious staring."

Though we disagreed neither was sure that his views could be relied upon. The dangers we might encounter the moment we stepped out of the Dans house and all along the way kept nagging at me despite the many good reasons I had advanced earlier for our taking such a step. And to think we had yet to face the sentries at the city boundary lines! My wife, on the other hand, who had first opposed this trip, feared that should Yang's guidance have come from the Lord, it would be a terrible mistake to reject it.

We both decided to call on God to resolve our dilemma.

## CHAPTER THIRTEEN

✥

## JOY UNDER THE SUN

> *. . . weeping may endure for a
> night but joy cometh in the morn-
> ing.*
>
> Psalm 30:5

When I left the Ipo hills with Yang and returned to the city, the
move had looked dangerous and unwise. Right then we learned
to depend not on how men judge a proposed course of action,
but on how God looks at it. We felt we should surrender our wills
to God's will, entirely and unconditionally.

"Dear Lord, I do not want to go with the children to the hills,"
my wife made her appeal as we both knelt down in prayer. "But
it is not for me to decide. Whatever Thou sayest, we shall follow." I, too, pleaded I would not insist on my own way.

During the meditation we read *God Calling,* a book we used
for our daily life. This message struck our attention:

> *From darkness into light,*
> *From uncertainty to certainty,*
> *And from disorder to order.*

Our continued stay in the city would mean darkness, uncertainty, and disorder; our departure to the hills would mean
light, certainty, and order. My wife shared my interpretation,
and we both were deeply impressed.

We then were guided to read the Bible, and the story of Nehe-
miah's journey to Judah appeared before us. The phrase, "May

85

let me pass through" cleared my doubt and my anxiety over the possibility of crossing the sentry lines between Manila and the neighboring hilly provinces.

Earnestly, my wife and I beseeched God for a specific assurance, such as the one I had received a year before at the time of my return to the city from Ipo.

We were again guided to open the Bible, and we caught our breath as we read:

> Live joyfully with the wife whom thou lovest all the days of the life of thy vanity, which He hath given thee under the sun.
>
> Ecclesiastes 9:9

"Under the sun"! For a year we had been deprived of sunshine. "By God's grace," I exclaimed, "we shall enjoy life together in the open wilderness under the sun."

Henceforth, Fely took the firm stand that we should go to the hills. It was one of her hardest spiritual struggles, and she came out with absolute obedience. No one foresaw that all the places in the city where my family and I had stayed would soon be raided, one after the other. Had we failed to follow the guidance, we would never have escaped the enemy's snares.

Living in faith was a wonderful experience, for there were times when we had to be patient and there were obstacles from within and from without that we had to overcome. Our struggle to carry out God's guidance lasted three months.

First, we had to convince our friends.

We could count on Aqui's support on our trip, but we doubted whether the Danses would understand. They had come to love our children dearly and whenever Sister Rosario went out, my wife would take care of Bachy just as if she were ours. We had enjoyed each other's fellowship and had become as one big family. It was hard for us to broach the subject to them.

At first Sister Rosario thought that we were getting tired of staying with them. I told them that my wife had strongly opposed the idea at the beginning but that finally we had submitted our-

86

selves to faith. Tito and Sister Rosario then suggested that we consult Mother Stagg and her two American lady missionary friends. We urged them to do so for us.

"They all think the jungle is no place for the children," Sister Rosario reported when she returned. "They pointed out that since Tony is in the enemy's hands, he may be forced to reveal your hiding place in the Ipo hills. This would lead to your capture." The missionary ladies loved us sincerely; we could not ignore their kind advice.

"Let us wait and see," my wife calmly said. Aqui was then in Mindoro, attending to his work. We could not do anything but wait.

"Delay does not mean denial." We were encouraged when we came across this quotation in *God Calling* during our daily meditation. After a month, Aqui returned to the city and visited us. Courageous as ever, he offered to send Rebecca and her three children—Linda, Eddie, and Boying—together with old Impo, ahead of us to Ipo. He also offered to send for his nephew Bayani Garcia, elder brother of Ruben, to clear the jungle where Camp Hope had once stood. A big grass house would be built for Yang's family and ours.

"Bayani will stay in Camp Hope and serve you. He will follow your orders in the jungle; his honesty and ability can be trusted," Aqui assured us. We agreed to this plan.

Another month passed. Yang came to us secretly again with his wife and two boys, Arthur and little Benny. They stayed for two days to plan the trip with us. I showed Yang what I had read in the Bible:

> Ye shall not go out with haste, nor go by flight, for the Lord will go before you; and the God of Israel will be your rereward.
>
> Isaiah 52:12

"We shall go to the mountains, but not with haste," I said. However, I asked him to have everything in readiness.

Two weeks after the Yangs had returned to the Lazos, I was guided to repeat my reading in Isaiah. Surprisingly, only then did this particular verse catch my attention:

> Depart ye, depart ye,
> go ye out from thence.

Isaiah 52:11

The time had come. The urge for us to depart rang in my ears. But how?

"I cannot understand why you people must leave the city. However, I am convinced God has opened the way for you," Sister Rosario remarked upon her return from the church the following day. She then told us the message from Mother Stagg.

Mother Stagg had come to favor our departure. She told Sister Rosario that in her hours of meditation, her fears for our trip to the mountains had vanished, and she was now distinctly guided to advise us to leave the city.

The day after that Sister Rosario had an errand to do at the Emmanuel Hospital. But soon she was back to tell us, almost breathlessly, "The two other lady missionaries in their quiet hour have also been guided to entreat you to leave the city quickly." She thus brought us, unsolicited, another message that we had been waiting for. "Dr. Darby even insists that you proceed to the hills without losing a single hour," Sister Rosario said.

The missionary ladies had discarded their former opinion, and even Sister Rosario and Tito were now convinced that our leaving the city was God's will.

The guidance received by all of us tallied. The ways in which we received it were different, but we had come to one and the same conclusion.

Dr. Darby, Miss Wilk, and Mother Stagg sought guidance during their quiet hour. They picked up divine messages as they put their receiving set in order. Sister Rosario and Tito sought guidance by trusting God to open the way. They believed God would take full responsibility without their having to worry about it themselves. In our hunted life the Yangs, my wife, and I sought guidance according to the circumstances. We would pray and seek messages in the Bible; we would trust God to open the way; we would put ourselves ready to receive divine thoughts through whatever way God should choose. God has set no condition except that we put implicit trust and belief in Him. "According to your faith, be it unto you." The way matters not; faith alone counts.

We were to leave the city for the Ipo hills. The question now before us was how we should go there.

Ipo is a high, rocky region about 32 miles northeast of Manila, linked with a chain of mountains extending eastward to the Sierra Madre range flanking the Pacific Ocean. Before the war, it could be reached in about an hour's drive by car from the city. But during the occupation, transportation facilities were abnormal. Civilians found it extremely difficult to leave the city and travel about. The enemy had commandeered all trucks, and gasoline was strictly rationed. Cars and trucks were not available, and had there been any, they would have attracted attention. To take the bus would mean to expose ourselves to the eyes of the crowd. Carabao carts were out of the question and too slow. Although horse rigs were preferable, it would be difficult to hide our identity from the rig owners, to say nothing of the drivers.

Aqui had a horse rig which he drove himself, but his horse was sick and weak. The rig, too, was a dilapidated thing and could accommodate only two passengers and a driver. We needed two more horse rigs. Where could we get them?

"Since it's God's will, He will provide," my wife remarked at our prayer meeting.

"I believe June 4 is the day you should leave for the hills," Sister Rosario suddenly remarked. She believed she was definitely guided to say so. She did not explain further and we accepted her word without question.

Strange things began to happen. A man named William Ghent, newly engaged in the horse rig business, frequented the Cosmopolitan Student Church. During one of his visits, on

June 3, 1943, Mother Stagg asked him, "Do you want to do a good turn to help some people?"

"Yes, Mrs. Stagg," Ghent replied.

"Then ask no questions. Just send two horse rigs early tomorrow morning to the yard in front of the Singalong Catholic Church which adjoins the Paco district."

Ghent nodded. He understood the nature of such an assignment. "I shall not fail to send them at five a.m. tomorrow," he said. "I will order my drivers to leave as soon as your men approach the church. Please ask the other party to send their own drivers. This will ensure that I and my drivers will know nothing about them."

Mother Stagg informed Tito of the plan. He rushed home with the good news. We all rejoiced.

Yang and Eva and their two boys, Arthur and Benny, moved their things that night from the Lazos' to the Dans house. With three families together, it looked like quite a big occasion. That night we held a big prayer meeting. We all got up early the next morning, excited and eager to face a new adventure.

Tito had an old friend who was a professional rig driver. He had sent for him and his son to drive for us. At five o'clock on the morning of June 4, 1943, Ghent's horse rigs arrived punctually in front of the Catholic church. As arranged, the drivers left as soon as our own men approached.

Aqui brought his sick horse and dilapidated rig, too. He had reckoned we would make Ipo in about six hours. We had eaten breakfast and had prepared a lunch in case we should not reach Ipo by noon.

Miss Wilk had asked Dr. Luz Nejal Bañez, a close friend of hers, to fashion a set of false teeth for me to wear on top of my own. It would pull my face down, make my eyes bulge, lengthen my lips, and enlarge my mouth. It was a good disguise!

I wore a *barong tagalog,* a Filipino native shirt, and sat at the rear, holding a huge earthen jar to cover me partially. Max Lazo sat beside me while Aqui took the driver's seat and held the reins. We tied an empty chicken crate behind and looked like typical farmers returning to the mountains.

Sister Martha, her two younger daughters—Priscilla and Amelia—Tito, the Yangs, my family, and our amah sat in Ghent's two rigs. Mario, a young escaped prisoner, also accompanied us. He had been sent by Mother Stagg to join us. He was a complete stranger to us, but we did not question him. Though it would be a long, strenuous, and extremely dangerous trip, our greathearted Filipino friends had volunteered to accompany us and act as a camouflage.

The streets were deserted at this early hour. Only Filipino MP's kept guard at the Balintawak check point when our rig approached.

Posting garrisons at boundaries was one way the Occupation Army took to prevent any undesirable element from freely going in and out of the city. "How many were caught at this point?" I wondered. The false teeth I wore over my own could be troublesome once I began answering questions. My Chinese accent, too, could easily be detected. But we were at the point of no return.

"Get down with Max. We have to be inspected," Aqui told us.

As we stood in line awaiting our turn, one of the MP's hailed us. We did not know what this could mean. "You can go ahead," the man shouted impatiently, not bothering to give us even a second glance.

Here I was, a man long wanted by the enemy, ordered curtly to pass through the sentry without even being touched by the guards! This, indeed, was little short of a miracle. The rig carrying my wife, Eva, and some of our children was cleared, too.

The MP's suddenly changed their attitude at the approach of the third rig, in which Yang rode. They stopped it and started to inspect it. Yang alighted and stepped aside, while Sister Martha faced the sentry's questioning.

"Where is your permit?" queried the MP.

"What permit do you mean?" Sister Martha asked.

"Don't you know the standing order of the military authorities that any family leaving the city for the provinces should obtain a permit from them?" the MP said. Knowing this order, they had yet allowed our other two rigs to pass unmolested and picked only on this one in which Sister Martha sat, facing them courageously. Being a Filipino, she was in a position to plead with the Filipino MP's, who had sympathy for their countrymen. She feigned ignorance of the new regulation and begged for consideration, pointing to her big group of children. The rig was finally allowed to proceed.

We left June 4, 1943, at the time when sentry regulations were somewhat relaxed. One day later would have meant disaster. For on June 5, Dr. Jose P. Laurel, who later became the Occupation President of the Philippines, was the victim of an assassination attempt. The Japanese Army immediately tightened its security measures. Heavily armed guards reinforced the sentry lines. Civilians were searched and questioned thoroughly, many being detained for further investigation.

Within a few days the secretary of the enemy-sponsored Philippine-Chinese Association was assassinated. And soon afterward, the vice-president of the association, the one who had spoken over the Japanese-controlled broadcasting station the day Corregidor fell, died at the hands of Chinese guerrillas. The enemy, enraged, stepped up their search for the resistance leaders.

## CHAPTER FOURTEEN

◈

## A GLORIOUS JOURNEY

*The birds had escaped the hunter's arrow, but flew away not without terror.*

Chinese Adage

Though we had crossed the city limits, we dared not look back but kept our faces toward the north.

Whipped into a brisk pace, Ghent's two strong horses soon overtook the sickly nag that pulled Aqui, Max, and me. We watched them speed ahead of us with joy, for now all three rigs had safely crossed the border.

Before long our rig began to catch up with them. The two other rigs had stopped at the roadside. The rig in the lead, bearing my wife, Eva, Tito, and some of our children, had met an accident. Rounding the first curve, their horse had stumbled, upsetting the rig and spilling everybody out, one on top of the other—with my wife underneath. She fainted, still clutching our little Andrew to her bosom. Upon regaining consciousness, she asked, "Are the children hurt?"

"No, they are all right. How do you feel, yourself?" asked Tito.

"Thank God the rig fell over on the side I was sitting on. If it had fallen the other way, little Benny would have been badly hurt," she said smiling. Her head and back showed black-and-blue bruises.

"Poor Fely, how much she has to suffer for me," I said to myself as I helped her up into the rig again. We were now in the province of Rizal. There were houses along the highway and we could not afford to create a scene. Hurriedly we picked up the broken kitchenware which had been scattered around and continued our journey.

Following the same route Yang, Tony, and I had traveled on the last day of 1941, we turned northeast to the Bulacan mountain region—a peaceful wilderness far from the turmoil of the city. I recalled a psalm:

> Oh that I had wings like a dove!
>> For then would I fly away, and be at rest.
> Lo, then would I wander far off,
>> And remain in the wilderness.
>
> Psalm 55:6, 7

Green hills surrounded us, and beyond lay barren fields. We stopped for lunch. Our children jumped from the rigs, beaming with joy as they breathed once more the fresh air they had missed for fourteen months. Everyone ate heartily, forgetting—for the time being—the tedious journey ahead.

Aqui fed his nag. "This horse was sick for two days and refused to eat. He was not fit for highway travel. I was sure he would die on reaching Ipo, but he has even galloped and has eaten much. He does not look sick anymore. Most unusual," Aqui said.

"The horse will not die even after reaching Ipo," I replied with full trust.

The children fluttered about like butterflies, plucking wild flowers and discovering one delight after another. Cecilie busied herself carrying our dishes back and forth. Unexpectedly, she stumbled and a thorn scratched her right leg. While blood was oozing out of the foot-long wound, she bit her lips, trying to keep back the tears. One could imagine what these children would have to undergo in the jungle.

We resumed our journey after an hour or more. Aqui had failed to consider the problem of crossing the rivers and creeks, whose bridges had been destroyed. This upset our schedule. At the first river, our children splashed in the water and bubbled with joy. But one river after another became monotonous and increased the strain on the horses. Each time we crossed a river, we had to pause to give them some rest.

We could not compute how long it took us to push through a mile. We only knew that every new step taxed the strength of our horses. There were no more cheerful looks. One thought filled our minds: Could we reach our destination? We seemed lost in a no-man's-land. It was near this area that Tony, Yang, and I had been arrested in our first flight to Ipo.

The sun was about to set, and we had covered only a little over half the way. As we moved further north, wider rivers challenged us. The horses could barely continue. To lighten the load some of the men carried the children while others helped push the rigs.

Showers fell, making the road muddy and slippery. Going around a curve, one of our rigs almost slipped over the edge of a cliff. But we kept on. We had spent 12 hours on the journey and we were still one-third of the way from Ipo. The children gave in to hunger and weariness, the younger ones weeping loudly.

The night grew darker, the road harder. Then, from sheer weariness, the horses came to a standstill. As a last resort, we asked the women to get down from the vehicles. But the horses wouldn't budge. Tito and Aqui confessed it was beyond human power to do anything further.

"We all have come to the end of our endurance," Tito sighed.

"And the horses are exhausted too," Aqui added.

"No, we simply cannot go any farther."

When the self-reliant Aqui admitted defeat and when the sturdy, optimistic Tito groaned helplessly, what hope could there be?

The showers got heavier. These thoughts crossed my mind: Should we stop here and expose our children to the dangers of the jungle? What if farmers should come our way early in the morning and see us in such a condition; would it not arouse their suspicion? What if a Japanese scouting party should happen to pass by and find us? Could we call off the trip to Ipo and return to the city now?

It was like riding on a tiger's back. It was safe neither to proceed nor to turn back. Clearly, we had come face to face with another test in faith.

I asked Tito and Aqui to join me in prayer. I prayed, "Loving Heavenly Father, the journey surely cannot end in this way. It was under Thy holy guidance that we took this trip and we firmly believed Thou were taking full responsibility. We know Thou are steadfast. The strength of man and horse has ended in exhaustion and we admit our complete helplessness. But man's impossibility is Thy possibility. O God, strengthen our faith and carry us onward. In the name of our Lord Jesus Christ."

Our voices blended in a fervent "Amen." I believed our prayer was heard. I ran a few steps farther so as to reach the rest of our scattered party and asked them to join me in another prayer.

I asked the drivers and the women and children to get in the rigs. "Everybody in his rig!" I shouted. "No need to unload anything. Let it be as it was when we left the city." Our women obeyed quickly. Our men followed silently. The two drivers reluctantly pulled the reins.

The first horse started! The second followed! I patted the horses and whispered, "You, too, are God's creatures. You must continue doing your part." The horses seemed to understand and fell into a steady trot. I ran back to Aqui and his sick horse. "The two other rigs are moving on," I yelled. Aqui lost no time in starting his poor, brave nag into a gallop. The horses climbed Apogan Cliff, the steepest section in Ipo, without any aid.

Sister Martha, barefooted and carrying a lamp, walked ahead to guide the first rig. The other two did not have sufficient light, and a slight slip could cause them to topple from the cliff.

"We need more light," someone shouted.

Deep in the rocky valley, with no other humans but ourselves, who could provide the much needed light? My wife remembered that Mother Stagg had given her an old flashlight with some used batteries. She had brought this along for the children to play with. She prayed and switched it on. It lit!

Everyone sang, "Glory, glory, Halleluiah, His truth is marching on!" Max and Tito, so nearly exhausted a while back, sang heartily as the rigs kept moving. The atmosphere of defeat had changed to one of triumph. No more pushing the rigs from behind, no more pauses to rest the horses. The stormy sky changed to a starry heaven.

> Have I not commanded thee? Be strong and of good courage; be not afraid, neither be thou dismayed: for the Lord thy God is with thee whithersoever thou goest.
>
> Joshua 1:9

"We have reached our destination," Aqui shouted.

The sturdy, little wooden house where Sister Martha had welcomed Tony, Yang, and me in the presence of the San Jose Police—almost one and a half years before—stood in the tall, wild grass off the highway.

"Is this the house?" my wife inquired, pointing the flashlight toward the house.

"Yes," Tito answered.

At this instant the flashlight went out. No amount of manipulating could make it light again. God provides enough, no more and no less.

It had taken us eighteen hours to reach our destination— three times what Aqui had calculated. The experience in faith had more than compensated for all the perils of the journey.

A battle and a victory indeed!

# CHAPTER FIFTEEN

❧❦❧

## CAMP HOPE AGAIN

*Thou art my hiding place; Thou*
*shalt preserve me from trouble;*
*Thou shalt compass me about*
*with songs of deliverance.*

Psalm 32:7

The northerly winds which greeted Yang and me on our first flight from Manila had not yet returned. The midnight silence of the little hilly village was broken only by the hoofbeats of our horses. Old Impo, Rebecca, Bayani, and Ruben rushed out to welcome us. It was an ideal hour to arrive, for the neighbors were sound asleep. The arrival of three rigs bearing more than twenty men, women, and children could have created a sensation among the mountain folk.

Impo immediately prepared food, but the children were too sleepy to eat. Since there were no beds, Eva, my wife, and our amah each took a corner of the hut and spread our mats. Our weary families soon settled down for the night, except for Yang and me, who remained at the table. Regaining my usual appetite, I finished three heaping plates of rice, ten bowls of *salabat* (native ginger tea), and some green mangoes. Yang ate heartily, too.

We were both in the highest of spirits. We recalled our adventures from the time we were arrested in San Jose up to only a few hours before, when both man and beasts had given in to despair. To relive our experiences was to count again the many blessings God had showered upon us. "Eighteen months have passed," I said. "Rather than saying that we have suffered that long, we shall say that we have obtained that much spiritual gain." Yang nodded in assent.

"And, to look forward, it seems we have a long, long way to go yet," he added.

"Exactly, God carries us through one trial after another to help us grow in faith and to prepare us to face the unknown future," I remarked. Yang nodded again. We finally lay down in a space near the table and drew a blanket over us. The birds could have complained that our loud snoring disturbed their morning choir!

We were up by daylight. Tito, Max, and the drivers left us with Ghent's two rigs, as had been previously arranged. Aqui and Sister Martha set out with the women and children along the jungle trail to Camp Hope, leaving Yang and me inside the wooden house. To prevent the mountain folk from knowing that the same Chinese refugees had returned, we were to wait until dusk before stepping out.

We took the occasion to chat with Impo and Rebecca, whom we called Becky. Young and pretty, Becky was the elder of the Aquino twins—Becky and Elizabeth. Courageous as her father, she had brought her three small children—Linda, Eddie, and the new baby, Boying—to the hills to comply with her father's wish. Her husband had to work in the city.

"Don't you find mountain work hard?" I asked her.

"No. My father loves this place, and I like to stay away from the city, too," Becky answered. "It is your families who are not used to the hills; they will meet hardships here." She assured us that she would do her part to help us whenever she could.

It was raining heavily that afternoon when Ruben and Bayani came from the jungle to lead us to camp. The two brothers had been working the whole day to finish the big hut in Camp Hope, which Aqui had offered to build two months before. As we were about to leave, Impo cautioned, "Don't go while it is raining." She knew the way would be difficult for us and feared we might not be able to stand the trip. Ordinarily, of course, we would not have risked it, but this was an emergency.

"The rain will prevent us from being seen by other people," I said to the good old lady.

We set out with Ruben and Bayani. The trail, covered with thorns and grass, was so muddy and slippery that I fell time and again. At length I spotted a light through the dense vegetation.

"Sir, the light comes from a place where the carabao used to be corralled," Ruben remarked. "It was deserted by some people fifteen months ago." This was all Ruben knew and could describe of the old Camp Hope, our former refuge and our present destination. At one time Aqui actually had kept his livestock there. I smiled. Fifteen months ago we had left the camp. Now I saw it again with my family there before me.

Yang had arrived at the camp ahead of Bayani, Ruben, and me. As he and Aqui greeted me, I held them with my muddy hands.

Camp I, the Aquinos' little nipa house, still stood, but many parts of it had been attacked by white ants. Camp II, the small hut Tony, Yang, and I used to squeeze into, had been torn down.

The newly built big hut, composed of grass roof and walls, was not at all as we had wanted it to be: It had neither kitchen nor doors, and the walls were so thin that the wind threatened to blow them down. It did not seem a fit place for women and children to live in.

Aqui told us that when he had asked Ruben and Bayani to put it up, he had advised them to economize as much as possible on the materials. They had even removed the boards from the ceiling of Aqui's roadside house and used them as our flooring.

Inside the big hut water dripped from leaks in the roof, and the wind came in gusts through the open spaces. In the dark, surrounding jungle, trees and plants were tossed and buffeted by lashing winds and rain. In a corner a coconut-oil lamp flickered.

What a miserable sight!

Mosquito nets, however, had been put up in separate places where our families were preparing for bed—which was, of course, on the floor.

Wet and dirty, I approached the corner where my wife was putting Andrew to sleep. She was weeping. "Fely," I said, "I am sorry, but there is no turning back."

While the children slept, we gathered for our devotion and smiled as Bayani sang "Silent Night" wearing Sister Martha's nightgown. He had been soaked to the skin and did not have a change of clothes. Each of us said a brief prayer. Calmness returned, the rain let up, and we passed the night.

Aqui left for Manila the following day. Sister Martha and her two daughters, Priscilla and Amelia, stayed in old Camp I to keep us company. Life in Camp Hope had been hard for Yang and me when we were by ourselves fifteen months ago; it was even harder for our families now.

We had to fight swarms of mosquitos and the women and children suffered from skin diseases and lice. My wife slipped and fell down frequently while carrying water from the well for our cooking and washing. Small tree trunks, loosely tied together by rattan vines, made up our kitchen floor. Still new to this swaying floor, Cecilie fell beside our clay stove which toppled over and spilled boiling water on both her thighs. Poor Cecilie tried to be brave.

Elsie, running toward Camp I one afternoon, tripped and fell face down over a jagged tree stump. Her right leg was impaled on a sharp projecting splinter. Innocently she tried to move her leg, which only made the spear-like splinter go deeper. The whole camp rushed to her as she screamed with pain. Big tears coursed down her cheeks as she watched the red blood gush from her wound. I helped her up gently, and my wife could only wash Elsie's wound with a decoction of guava leaves, our cure-all for wounds or skin diseases.

The walls of our cogon hut were attached to the upper beams only. One day, when Betty was carrying Benny on her back, she lost her balance just as she reached the door. Involuntarily, she leaned on a hanging wall for support. Both children fell out of the hut. Although our floor was only a yard above the ground, they received a severe shock.

One evening, while at supper, we were besieged by an army of winged ants—millions of them.

"Mama, I think I ate two flying ants!" Benny Boy shouted. The children, with hands covering their ears, scampered here and there, jumping up and down trying to escape the pests. I asked them to get inside the mosquito nets, and our men built a big bonfire in front of our hut. In a few minutes the winged invaders became part of the ashes. The children popped out of the mosquito nets and rushed back to their places.

"Our food is full of dead ants!" Andrew exclaimed in disgust.

To keep alive meant to struggle. Like pioneers we organized, mobilizing our efforts, and soon found that each had something to contribute. Mario, the stranger Mother Stagg had sent to us, had been raised in the mountains. He felt completely at home in the jungle, climbing trees and steep hills with great agility and bringing home many kinds of wild fruits. He was invaluable. Bayani, formerly a trade-school teacher, was adept with tools. Yang, an engineering graduate of the University of the Philippines, directed Bayani and Ruben in improving the big hut. One of my daily chores was to gather firewood in the forest with the children. I climbed the trees and allowed my heavy weight to bend them over so the children could break off the dry branches.

We cut a small secret trail from Camp Hope to the backyard of the Aquinos' roadside house. Becky would reach us through this passage to inform us of news that came her way. I named the trail "Rebecca Road." We also erected a wooden bridge, linking Camp Hope with Rebecca Road. Since Bayani built it, I named it "Bayani Bridge."

Tito visited us often from Manila. He was a farmer's son, and he taught us how to make use of *buho* (native bamboo) as pipe lines. Our pipes stretched over a quarter of a mile, from the spring over the hill to our camp. Thus we had a natural supply of water coming over what I called the "Tito Water System." We put up a chicken coop named after our Louisa and a bamboo sty for the pigs, called "Pepe's Pig Pen." Pepe was Yang's nickname.

A hundred yards from our grass hut we cleared a beautiful

spot where wild orchids grew protected by an ancient alibang-bang tree. The *alibangbang* tree is a native tree with thick foliage and looks massive. Its height approximates that of a mango tree. It is a favorite habitat of beetles. Here Yang and I had undergone our first fast, in 1942. I called it the "Mary Hawthorne Helen Orchid Garden" in honor of the three missionaries. Nearby, we erected a tabernacle for our chapel, which I named "Martha Chapel" to express our admiration for Sister Martha's faith. Sister Martha appreciated the idea but objected to the name.

"I don't deserve the honor. If you insist on naming the chapel 'Martha Chapel,' we should consider it as being named after the Martha you loved who is now by our Lord's side," she said, referring to our beloved baby, Felisa Martha. Then she added, "It is generally accepted that a chapel is named after someone who has passed away." We stuck to the name despite her objection, which we took as modesty. We had no idea then that Sister Martha's sacrifice afterward would prove her explanation to be a prophecy.

We cut down more trees, dug up the roots, and burned them for fertilizer. We cultivated a farm and garden and widened the clearing around us. Yang and I, like the Filipino members of the camp, became adept at using boloes and hoes. Our women and children also took interest in raising food. I would name a vegetable after the one who planted and took care of it. So we had Fely's and Eva's *sitao* (string beans), Cecilie and Benny's pumpkin, Arthur and Elsie's *upo* (a type of squash), Dorcie and Andrew's tomatoes, and Betty's okra. Our enthusiasm in planting and caring for these crops and our anticipation before they could be harvested made us eat them with relish and fun.

At harvest time, Cecilie and Benny Boy ran eagerly to their pumpkin field. They returned disappointed, carrying in their hands one empty pumpkin shell. In the whole field only one pumpkin had grown. How indignant they were when they found that white ants had beaten them to it and eaten the core, leaving only the shell!

The children discovered something new and exciting each

day. One day it was a flying lizard. Another day it was a deadly bout between a snake and three rats on the roof of Camp I.

"The long brown snake fought very hard, but he died," Elsie said.

"The three big rats also died from snake bites," Arthur added excitedly.

"Yes, they fought quite a battle, but they all died in the end," Dorcie said.

Aqui had brought along two turkeys—a male and a female. At feeding time one day the children discovered that "Mr. and Mrs. Turk" were absent. Excitedly, they started looking for their winged friends, but to no avail. A whole week passed. Still no news. Then one afternoon the children found them sitting on two nests in a hidden ravine. Each sat on five eggs.

"We found Mr. and Mrs. Turk—they are hatching baby turkeys!" Dorcie shouted. A few weeks later, the turkeys came home with "Junior" and his sister. The children ran to the nests and found eight unhatched eggs.

"Not a single one sat on by Mr. Turk hatched. But it was sweet of him to keep Mrs. Turk company," Betty reported.

One afternoon a hawk flew away with one of our baby turkeys. The children rushed out, straining their necks to follow the "big bad bird." Their eyes were wet with tears.

Yang and I hid in the forest almost every afternoon. There we would read or discuss our situation. Because of the dampness, we would build a small fire which also helped our wives to locate us. Somehow, the children got wise to where we were, and from then on they would always seek us out, trailing us by the smoke.

The spot where I used to meditate during the early days of the occupation and where I sought God's deliverance after I had heard Dominador's report that the enemy would shoot me on sight—this became Yang's and my favorite nook. There, the children would climb a thriving old tree whose trunk had been pushed to the ground by typhoons, and they would while away the afternoon lying on its sturdy branches, teasing each other or eating guavas plucked from the trees around.

In the forest anthills were a common sight. We would destroy a hill one day only to find it rebuilt the next. "Yes, the perseverance of the ants is admirable," I told the children, hoping that we might have the same determination.

We learned to subsist in the jungle as the Swiss family Robinson had done a long time before.

The children looked forward to Sunday especially. They would get up early, put on their clean Sunday best, and run ahead of us to the chapel. Yang and I would take turns in delivering the sermon. Threatened with capture though we were, we could preach more freely to our audience than the preachers in the occupied cities. The jungle echoed with the full-throated voices of our children, who sang straight from their innocent hearts. There was a song on everybody's lips.

> Thou art my hiding place; Thou shalt preserve me
> from trouble; Thou shalt compass me about with songs
> of deliverance.
>
> Psalm 32:7

Although we lived deep in the jungle, strangers would occasionally pass near our place. Our signal was to sing "Bahay Kubo" (My Nipa Hut), which meant that everyone should take cover. Tito and Max visited us quite often. They told us they could hear our songs from a distance. "Each trip we make to Camp Hope exhausts us," Tito remarked, "but each time we reach our city homes, we long to be back with you, to participate in this wonderful spiritual atmosphere."

Sister Martha stayed with us for three months. She helped our women adjust themselves to mountain life. After her return to the city with Priscilla and Amelia, she wrote us:

Beloved:
    At first I thought without us you would never be able to get along in the hills. Now I realized you do not depend on men. It is on God and God alone that you de-

pend. We may all have departed from you but God re-
mains with you always.

Affectionately,<br>Martha

We were awakened one night by the barking of our dogs. Sister
Rosario had come to visit us for the first time. During her short
stay she would go out to the fields with the children to gather
food.

" 'Give us this day our daily bread.' The Lord's Prayer has
become a reality," said Sister Rosario. "I came to comfort you,
but it was I who was comforted. Your life at Camp Hope with
God supplying your daily needs shows that He still drops manna
for His people."

In October 1943, after she had returned to the city, Sister
Rosario sent her niece Araceli Marcelino, whom we called Lily,
to stay with us at Camp Hope. Lily continued to give English
lessons to our children.

"Dr. Darby and Miss Wilk were thrilled to hear how well you
are carrying on," said Tito, who had accompanied Lily. "They
want to come but realize the impossibility. They asked me to
tell you that though you have to struggle for physical existence,
spiritually you are living next to Heaven."

If we had our moments of strength, we also had our moments
of weakness. When the days clouded over and rain filled the night,
impatiently we waited for MacArthur's return. Facing east, I
could imagine behind the blue hills the Pacific Ocean, over which
MacArthur and his armed forces would come. Just as that great
sea ebbed and swelled, our hope of redemption surged and
retreated. Every afternoon I would sing a lullaby and cuddle
my little Andrew to sleep. I did not know how to sing but the
sounds I made helped to unburden my grieving heart.

One afternoon Bataan and Barker, our dogs, interrupted my
lullaby with excited barks. They had discovered a multi-colored
wild tomcat on our papaya tree. Somehow Mario killed the cat
and cooked it for his lunch, so great was his hunger. He never
told us how he did it. All he said was, "I ate the tomcat." After

that, for many nights when the clouds veiled the moon, we could hear a lonely yowl. It was a female wild cat near the papaya tree, searching for her missing mate.

We felt sorry Mario had not spared the tomcat's life.

> The fox mourns the death of the rabbit, for the same
> fate could happen to him.

This Chinese adage expressed my sentiment toward the tomcat. We had been chased—like the tomcat—and were still poised for flight.

# CHAPTER SIXTEEN

❦

## TEMPTATION TO SURRENDER

*The brisk breeze reveals the sturdy grass; tumultuous times bring out the loyal souls.*
Chinese Adage

A November typhoon lashed Camp Hope one night. The clashing of trees and the pouring rain matched the ferocity of the gale, making us feel as if the hill itself were about to fall on our flimsy hut. The children held tightly to one another. Morning found our hut still standing, but our plants had been mercilessly blown down and many completely ruined.

It rained continuously, for it was the typhoon season. Camp Hope became very damp. I had contracted bronchitis, which was aggravated by the foul weather. The leaks in our grass roof became so bad that my wife and I had to get up nights to move our children around to keep them dry. Chilled by the cool breeze, I coughed almost incessantly. "God have pity," my wife would say.

"Think of the tortures and the misery the prisoners are experiencing at Fort Santiago. Isn't my condition much better compared to theirs? We have every reason to be thankful to God," I would reply. "If the enemy had caught me, I would have been killed a year and a half ago and would be only skull and bones by now." I deserved no pity. But pitiful were my children and my wife, who suffered on my account.

Like a ship on the ocean, our roof of matted grass, with its beams tied to the frame of the hut by split rattan, would bob up and down with the wind. We were always apprehensive that should a bigger blast come, the vines would give way, our roof would fly off, and we would be left exposed to the elements.

My wife woke me up one calm night. "Do you hear what I hear?" she asked. I recognized it as the swishing sound of a snake up on the roof. Was it snoring or singing? I mused.

Several nights we heard the same sound. Finally, one afternoon my wife saw the long tail of a green snake hanging in the room over the window sill; its head, which projected out of the window, was raised high with a frog in its mouth. My wife quickly called Louisa, who clubbed the snake on the head. Since it had the frog in its mouth, the snake could not move fast—nor could it harm anyone. Everybody gathered around the long body of the green snake, sprawled on the ground below the window. I was happy that there would be no more swishing sounds to disturb the sweet dreams of my wife—unless there were other snakes nestling in our grass roof.

The reptiles did not bother us further, but they took their toll of our animals. A pig then was worth a little fortune, and we had two of the precious creatures—until the day we found one of them dead inside the pig pen. Two fang marks were found on its neck. What a loss to us!

After two years of hardship, we were living in abject poverty. The American forces had pushed to Bismarck Island and thence to New Guinea, but my cough worsened faster than our allies advanced. One night, while I was brushing my teeth, my knees wobbled and I collapsed. "Even my knees refuse to support me," I sighed. No one was around. I pulled myself together, and dragged myself to my room. I lay down to count our days in exile. Twenty-three months had passed, each like a year.

Next day Sister Martha came to visit Camp Hope. Looking at my pallor and noticing my loss of weight, she refrained from talking with me about serious matters.

That evening, by the dim light of the small coconut-oil lamp, I noticed her whispering to Yang as they stood in a corner. By the way they glanced at me, I could tell they were speaking of me.

"Tell me, aren't you talking about my health?" I asked. Yang nodded. "You must have been discussing the idea that I might die." Their silence confirmed my suspicion. "You are both wrong," I said. "It is true that we cannot afford to have doctors and medicines and that we don't have enough daily nourishment. But we have God." Of course, I could not blame those who thought otherwise.

Every morning I would get my hoe and go out to the farm. The day after her arrival, Sister Martha approached me. "Brother Jimmy," she said, "you're not used to farming; you should take care not to overdo."

"I appreciate your kind attention, Sister, but do not worry about me. I am all right," I answered her in all sincerity. My physical condition could affect the morale of our camp; I must not weaken.

One morning, while I was harvesting the remnants of our vegetables, I heard someone crying bitterly among the bushes. It was Louisa. When she had come into the jungle with us, she had thought we would soon be liberated. With another Christmas approaching she began to despair, for she realized now that redemption was still far away. She also had noticed that my physical condition had deteriorated steadily. What if I should die or be captured? All these thoughts had so depressed her that she finally broke into hysterical sobs, shouting at the top of her voice that she wanted to leave.

I had no right to keep her; neither had I the heart to allow her to return to the city where she would face almost certain capture and torture. My wife and the Yangs could not find words to comfort her. After a while, however, the faithful amah came to her senses, dried her tears, and quietly resumed her duties.

The fear of our Cantonese amah regarding my possible capture was justified. Before leaving Camp Hope, Sister Martha whispered to me, "I certainly hate to disturb your peace of mind, but I feel you must know the actual situation. Mother Stagg has been told secretly by Pastor Chua of the Chinese Evangelical Church that spies carrying your picture have called at his church. It seems the enemy has been hunting for you with no letup." In fact, enemy spies had tried to gain information from most of our relatives and friends. Even my former colleague Vicente L. del Fierro was visited several times by both uniformed officers and plainclothesmen checking on me.

After Sister Martha left, my brother-in-law Amado was the next visitor to the camp. He brought disturbing news about my mother, saying that she had begun to barter her belongings for food. Mother Stagg had visited her. "My sight is failing and I am about to go blind," my mother had said to the good pastor. "I know it will not be possible for me to meet my son, but I do wish to see my grandchildren before I die." My mother held Mother Stagg's hands while tears fell upon them. Mother Stagg, deeply touched, thought of taking my mother to Ipo. She asked Amado to find out our opinion.

My father had died young. My mother was still very young. She remained a widow and lived in poverty. She cast all her hopes on me. Year after year she struggled on until I was old enough to support us. Now I had become a wanted man and had drifted away from her without letting her know of my whereabouts. Poor mother; though only in her middle fifties, due to her failing eyesight, she was most handicapped. I knew how much she had wanted to see all of us before she lost her sight completely.

But it was impossible for my mother to come to the hills. The hazardous trip would kill her.

My wife offered to make a trip with Amado to see her. It would have been a dangerous and foolhardy venture, however, and I could not give my consent.

I felt that I certainly had acted as an ungrateful son. Our hearts bled for my mother in her loneliness and sorrow.

Amado had another mission—a very important one.

"General Kuroda has granted amnesty to a number of people. Some Chinese leaders who were sentenced to long imprisonment during Homma's rule have been released on parole under the guarantee of the Japanese-sponsored Philippine-Chinese Association," Amado reported. "Tony is out of prison."

It was good to hear about our friend's release.

After a moment of hesitation, Amado opened the subject. "Go Colay, president of the association, has a proposition for you," he said.

Go Colay had contacted one of my cousins, and through him Amado was asked to relay to me the offer of amnesty.

"I believe the American forces will return to the Philippines one day. But this day may be several years from now," he confided to my cousin. "Even if Go Puan Seng succeeded in evading the Japanese, he could never live until the Americans return. He'll die of either hunger or disease in the mountain fastnesses. I am one of his closest townmates and in a position to arrange with the military authorities for him to surrender and I can secure his release. I have done it for others. Surely I shall do it for him."

Before my cousin left his office, he emphasized, "Ask him to think not of himself, but of his family."

Go Colay had guessed my physical condition correctly and he had hit the very core of my family problem. His offer of surrender could have sprung from two things: one, his own initiative to help me; and the other, an order from the Japanese Army. I had no way of judging the true source of the offer. But I knew that while others had to seek favors from him, he would be most happy to offer me help because we belonged to the same town back in China.

His entreaty that I surrender could not be interpreted as having the same intention as the note I had received through Mother Stagg from the Chinese spy in 1942. That note had offered inducements for me to give myself up in order to complete the list for the scheduled execution. The present offer was extended to me at a time when the Japanese authorities were seeking support from the people. Possibly my fellow townsman felt that since some other Chinese had surrendered after enduring a hunted life for a long time, I might follow their lead. The Japanese had established a Chinese daily newspaper in Manila, and they needed a publisher who had a name familiar to the community to boost their propaganda efforts. They could have thought of using me instead of killing me. Should I cooperate with them, I could relieve my family from hunger and hardship.

It was a period of moral degeneration. After two years of war, sensibilities had been blunted. Manila had become a center for traffic in opium and narcotics and for gambling, prostitution, speculation, and "buy-and-sell." There were those who made fortunes out of others' misfortunes.

> The brisk breeze reveals the sturdy grass; tumultuous times bring out the loyal souls.
>
> Chinese Adage

Worn out by poverty and sickness, I could have been tempted by the offer of amnesty now more than at any other time. "What do you think of the offer yourself?" I asked Amado. "Should I surrender now?"

"Mother Stagg thinks the president of the Chinese Association has a point in saying that your family should be considered," Amado said, refusing to commit himself.

The pitiful condition of my mother and the hardships suffered by my wife and our children certainly deserved every bit of my consideration. But my mother, who in chastity remained a widow all her life, certainly would not want her son to be a traitor. What honor could I bring my wife and our children were I to give in to the pressures of the enemy? Many of my friends who subscribed to the same principles I had, had been sacrificed and martyred. Could I do less? There were other friends who continued to fight for the cause I espoused and who were now carrying on the fight underground. Would not my surrender shatter their morale? How about the mass of people who attended public meetings at which I spoke, who read my editorials, and who had taken me as one of their symbols in the resistance movement? How would they feel should I surrender? Although to some my holding out meant little or had no significance, the least I could do was to hold out for the cause which I had advocated and for which I had demanded total sacrifice.

My wife and I knelt down to pray, looking up to our uncompromising Lord Jesus Christ, who had refused to say even a word to Pilate in spite of the cross before Him. We refused the offer to surrender. Let the enemy shoot us on sight. Let suffering and sickness be ours. Let the days of waiting be hard. But under no circumstance would we barter our faith and our loyalty. Amado, inspired by our decision, said it was what he had expected of us. Yang and his family assured us they would stick with us to the end.

> To whom we gave place by subjection, no, not for an hour.
>
> Galatians 2:5

# CHAPTER SEVENTEEN

❦

## JUNGLE CHRISTMAS

*Death by hunger is a minor thing; but the loss of one's character is a catastrophy.*
Chinese Adage

The offer for me to surrender came at the same time that a Philippine government was being organized with Dr. Jose P. Laurel at its head. Laurel was a close friend of Quezon and an independent dynamic leader for the Filipino cause.

"The setting up of the Laurel Government shows us that Japan now needs active help from the Filipino people," I said to Amado. "American advances in the Pacific might not be very rapid, but Japan is on the defensive. I can only analyze the war from a distance, but I am positive the day of liberation is not very far away." Yang shared my view.

Leaving our hills, Amado assured us he would consult Mother Stagg and would make sure that neither my cousin nor the officials of the Chinese Association would know contact had been made with me. My wife and I asked him to look after my mother.

Thinking that the enemy's wrath would be increased by my continued defiance and that the search for me would be intensified, I gathered my wife and children about me. I said, "With the opening of the second front in Europe, Germany is on the losing end. In the Pacific and on the Asia mainland, Japan has suffered great setbacks one after the other. Her total defeat is but a matter of time. Soon we shall all see victory." I paused a while and then continued. "No matter what may happen to your daddy

*115*

between now and liberation, my children, I am sure the day will come when you will be able to return home as loyal citizens to tell our friends—and even pass on to the next generation—the sufferings you have undergone with your daddy. You can be proud that we had not given in to the enemy."

My remark was rather passive. It could be taken as a last will to my daughters and son. The children were too young to understand. My wife disliked my negative attitude. "You need not imagine things and worry so much. All we shall do is trust God and struggle on," she said.

And struggle we did—especially to get the food to keep us alive. Our children's dresses were bartered for corn and livestock. I even traded my wife's dress for a wild pig which a neighboring farmer had snared and which we hoped to fatten. But, alas, the next morning we found only a piece of hempen rope still tied around the tree. Gone was my wife's dress, and gone the pig!

Rice was scarce. Not only in the hilly region but in Manila, too, the poor were eating *camotes* (sweet potatoes), cassava roots, and roasted coconuts. We had to ration rice and camotes, and we often substituted *butuan* for them, a sour banana full of seeds as big as beans. It was hard to swallow and it irritated the throat. Our children would ask for a small piece of *panocha* (caked brown sugar) to help them push the "stony bananas," as they called them, down their little throats. There were times when hunger would drive us to dig and scratch in the soil for any trace of camotes left unharvested until all hopes of finding even a small piece were gone. All the children, including my three-year-old boy, and Yang's little son Benny, would trail after me in this "camote hunt."

"Bayani said he has a friend who is working for the Japanese. The man has much influence and has offered to buy rice for him," Yang told me one afternoon. "Bayani is waiting for the money," continued Yang. I was happy at the news and told my wife to give Yang the money.

As Yang was about to step out of the hut, an old Chinese saying came to me: "Don't drink water from a thief's spring." I changed my mind and called Yang back.

"Why?" Yang inquired.

"Why do we refuse to surrender or collaborate and prefer to hold out here in the hills?" I asked. "Because we refuse to bow to the enemy. Because we want to stand by our principles. Why should we seek the help of a collaborator to obtain a few grains of rice?" I said. "No, my dear friend, let us rather tighten our belts."

Of course, no one would ever know we had done business with a collaborator in the jungle. But my conscience would not allow us to do so. I thought this over in silence, knowing well that my decision had deprived members of the camp of the food they craved.

> Death by hunger is a minor thing; but the loss of one's character is a catastrophy.
>
> Chinese Adage

It could have sounded stupid to some people. But it was for us to live it then. Yes, the cold winter will reveal the pine trees' virtue and endurance.

We managed to purchase still unharvested camotes by the plot from nearby farmers. We later followed an old Chinese custom—cutting the camotes into slices and drying them. Those who did the slicing had blisters on their hands and those who spread the slices out to dry were sunburned, with their skin peeling off like that of young potatoes.

Confucius once said about Yen Hui, one of his disciples who had lived in poverty all his life:

> Admirable indeed was the virtue of Hui! With a single bamboo dish of rice, a single gourd of drink and living in his mean narrow lane, while others could not have endured the distress, he did not allow his joy to be affected by it. Admirable indeed was the virtue of Hui!

Saint Paul said in his letter to the Philippians:

117

Not that I speak in respect of want: for I have learned, in whatsoever state I am, therewith to be content. I know both how to be abased, and I know how to abound: everywhere and in all things I am instructed both to be full and to be hungry, both to abound and to suffer need. I can do all things through Christ who strengthens me.

Philippians 4:11-13

It was with inexpressible satisfaction that we had weathered another hard, long year, and we came to gather around a big bonfire on Christmas Eve, 1943—our second Christmas in self-exile.

Though living in the wilderness, we were fired with the hope that surged in the shepherds watching for the Messiah in Bethlehem 2,000 years ago, and we poured out our joy in lilting cadences.

Aqui, Sister Martha, and their two younger daughters had come from the city to join us, and Tito and Amado reached the camp that evening.

On Christmas Day our children jumped and ran all about the hills. At our chapel Sister Martha directed a play. Betty was chosen to be the Virgin Mary. Arthur and Andrew acted as shepherds while Cecilie, Dorcie, Elsie, Priscilla, and Amelia portrayed the Heavenly Host.

The children wore new clothes cut out from curtains. But whatever the fabric had been, it would have looked beautiful on them. Their faces had brightened with the spirit of the occasion, for to children Christmas will always be the happiest event of the year, no matter where and how it is celebrated.

Our Christmas reunion was marred, however, by an unexpected incident. Aqui had brought along a young man, one Eduardo Marzan, who he wanted us to keep in the camp. Our pockets were about empty, and feeding eighteen to twenty persons daily was a big responsibility. With the price of commodities sky high, each mouth counted.

Our understanding with Aqui had been that he would con-

118

sult us first before bringing additional persons to the camp. Marzan was a complete surprise.

The young man, a friend of Aqui's son Ernesto, was in his early twenties. Even Aqui did not know much about his background. Because of the increasing unemployment in Manila, Ernesto had begged his father to give Marzan a place to stay. Yang and I thought we should not assume the burden.

Aqui persisted. "When you could not find a place, I took you in. Now I am taking this boy in," he had finally said. Yang was upset and I felt deeply offended.

Human relations are sometimes faulty, but God's care is perfect. Though we accepted Eddie Marzan with misgivings, he proved to be an indispensable help in the days to come.

Aqui left with Tito and Amado for the city, leaving Sister Martha and her two daughters to stay with us until the New Year. It was our family tradition to have a prayer meeting on New Year's Eve, to watch through the last hours of the old year and draw promises from the Bible for the New Year. Each person would draw from a tin box a Bible verse written on a paper slip. On the last day of 1943 I shut myself up to pray and select Bible promises. I opened the Bible at random, noting the best verses I came across. One by one I recorded them on slips of paper. Unexpectedly, I opened to the last page of Daniel. Searching the page from the top to the very end, I could not find any better verse than this one:

> Go thou thy way till the end be: For thou shalt rest, and stand in thy lot at the end of the days.
>
> Daniel 12:13

At the midnight drawing this one went to Sister Martha. It was a verse that promised blessings at the end, but the odd line "Thou shalt rest" gave everybody a vaguely uneasy feeling.

# CHAPTER EIGHTEEN

⋙⋘

## THE MASS ARRESTS

*Even the moaning of the winds,
the cries of the herons, the swaying trees and the rustling shrubs
resembled approaching enemy
soldiers. . . .*

Chinese Adage

The year 1944 was to be a crucial year. When Sister Martha took her two daughters back to the city after our New Year celebration, she was to face an experience as horrible as a nightmare.

An enemy agent, who professed to be an underground worker, had infiltrated the church group. Early in the year, Mother Stagg began to sense that her underground activities had leaked out. She hurriedly disposed of secret papers which she asked trusted church members to keep for her, Tito and Aqui among them. Other important documents, including a list of those who had contributed funds in exchange for guerrilla notes, were buried in the church backyard by Agustin, another escaped war prisoner who had taken over Mario's job.

Among the guerrilla leaders who had contact with Mother Stagg at that time was the Zambales resistance chief, Ramon Magsaysay. On the morning of January 28, the day Mother Stagg was taken by Japanese MP's, Magsaysay had an appointment with her. On his way to meet her Magsaysay saw the Cosmopolitan Student Church surrounded by Japanese MP's and decided not to go in. Had he done so, he would certainly have been captured.

Mother Stagg came with her husband, Dr. Samuel W. Stagg, to the Philippines in 1923. They had two sons, Lionel and Sam Boyd, and two daughters, Mary Ruth and Margaret Ann. Her husband, an outspoken preacher against Japanese aggression, had mysteriously absented himself from Manila, leaving her to carry on the missionary work. Mary Ruth, Margaret Ann, and Lionel had gone to the United States before Japan attacked Pearl Harbor. Only the younger boy, Sam Boyd, was by her side when the enemy seized the church. After her arrest, Sam was taken to the Santo Tomas internees' camp.

Emmanuel Hospital was raided at the same time as the church. Miss Wilk and Dr. Darby, together with Mother Stagg, were thrown into Fort Santiago. The boy, Agustin, was also arrested.

Next day, the enemy MP's surrounded the church again. They had brought Agustin with them and ordered him to unearth the documents buried in the backyard. With the papers were guns and a small quantity of ammunition. It was circulated among church members that the enemy had begun to focus their attention on Yang because his picture had been discovered among the documents.

Bayani, who had gone to the city to purchase commodities, rushed back to tell us the shocking news, adding, "Before I left, Uncle Aqui told me the situation was very tense and I must not be seen in the city anymore since I have been the one contacting Mother Stagg." We could imagine how the enemy would deal with these three lady missionaries. The American forces were too far away to rescue them, and the guerrillas were not in a position to break prison walls. We could only pray to God to sustain them with courage and fortitude.

We sent Bayani to his hometown, Baliuag, in Bulacan Province about fifteen miles from Ipo, to ask his brother Ruben, who had left Camp Hope some time ago, to make a trip to the city to obtain more information.

Bayani came back, pale and trembling. We knew the situation must have deteriorated still further, but it was worse than we had anticipated. His brother had returned to Baliuag and relayed to him the bad news that on February 2 the Aquino house in Manila had been raided and Aqui arrested. The same night, the Dans house was raided and Tito taken. He and Aqui had been tied and taken away in a military truck with many others. Samuel Huang, my newspaper's former cashier, was arrested for having subscribed to Mother Stagg's guerrilla notes. A mass arrest of members of the church followed. We could expect the long arm of the enemy to reach us any moment.

Max Lazo, who had sheltered the Yangs, was visiting us at the time and thus narrowly escaped arrest. He fled to Ilocos.

> Even the moaning of the winds, the cries of the herons, the swaying trees and the rustling shrubs resembled approaching enemy soldiers . . .
>
> Chinese Adage

The air we breathed seemed filled with fear. Not an inch of soil was safe. We recalled God's summons for us to depart from Manila to the hills. We had been told that there would be darkness, uncertainty, and disorder—all these had now come to pass.

"What we need is a Word from God," my wife said calmly. "So long as we have a Divine Promise to cling to, we need not be unduly frightened." The whole camp gathered to pray. God spoke to us in Psalm 124 as we opened the Bible:

> If it had not been the Lord
> who was on our side when
> men rose up against us;
> Then they would have swallowed
> us up quick, when their rod
> was kindled against us;
> Then the water had overwhelmed
> us, the stream had gone
> over our soul.
> Blessed be the Lord, who hath
> not given us as a prey to
> their teeth.
> Our soul is escaped as a bird

out of the snare of the
fowlers; the snare is
broken, and we are escaped,
Our help is in the name of the
Lord, who made heaven and
earth.

Word by word the Psalm described our precarious situation, for we were indeed like birds escaped from the snares of fowlers. Our hunted life had reached a crucial stage. With Mother Stagg, Dr. Darby, Miss Wilk, Tito, and Aqui captured, we were helplessly isolated—we had no one to depend on and nowhere else to go. We were then practically in the enemy's clutches. Our ability to make a final escape depended entirely on the help of our Lord, as promised in Psalm 124.

Zoning in the mountains followed the mass arrest. This measure was taken to force anti-Japanese elements to come out from hiding and, at the same time, to weaken the position of the guerrillas who had their bases in the hills.

"Everyone on this hill is leaving," panted old Impo, who had hurried from the roadside house to warn us. The mountain folk had been told that within 24 hours the enemy would shoot anyone found in the jungle. While the old lady was speaking, we could hear the sound of carreton wheels rolling over rough trails down to the highway. The mountain people had begun their exodus.

"We cannot go to town without exposing ourselves," I told Impo.

"But you have no other choice," the old lady insisted.

I called the group for a meeting. "This is an emergency on top of a calamity," I remarked. We placed full trust in the Lord's guidance as we opened the Bible. The following message came to us:

Thou wilt keep him in perfect peace, whose mind is stayed on thee: because he trusted in thee.

Isaiah 26:3

With this assurance, I was confident that the enemy's zoning would in no way disturb our peace. "We understand the situation and we appreciate your advice, but we will stay in the hills instead of running out in haste," I told Impo. "God is dependable. Let us not be alarmed."

Impo left, shaking her head.

All was quiet. Our neighbors had evacuated, leaving Camp Hope to its fate.

The zoning was to last three days. After that period, all those who had been ordered to leave the hills could return. Three days later carreton wheels were again heard rumbling over the roads. The mountain folk who had left in such haste were returning.

We had passed the crisis of the zoning.

On March 12, 1944, I was alone in the forest reading when my wife ran to me. and exclaimed, "The church tabernacle has fallen!"

This was our makeshift chapel on the hilltop. We had fashioned it out of branches of trees and vines. Its falling apart could have been a natural occurrence. But to my wife it was God's warning that Camp Hope was no longer safe.

We did not know then that two days before the tabernacle fell —on March 10, 1944—our escape to Ipo had been revealed to the enemy.

In the Ipo hills we saw nothing of the Japanese intelligence movement, but all the time enemy agents were hunting for us and sifting and evaluating the evidence and confessions gathered from the members of the church group who had been dragged to Fort Santiago as a result of the mass arrest. They were kept in separate cells between periods of torture and interrogation. A slip in answering made by one precipitated a battery of new questions fired at the others. The enemy then sorted out the various replies extracted through torture and relentless grilling.

Tito and thirty other persons were confined in a dirty 16-by-19-foot cell. After suffering for eight consecutive days without being given any food, he was brought to face the Japanese interrogator. Before the interrogation, he was flogged from head to foot. At times he was hung from the ceiling by his thumbs. At other times he was forced to kneel while holding a chair. A slight movement would prompt a rain of blows.

One day Tito happened to pass by the lady missionaries' cell. He saw Mother Stagg's face all swollen and black. Miss Wilk's looked even worse. At that moment Mother Stagg whispered to him, "It's no use. They know everything. You may tell them what you know."

Tito wept.

Aqui, who knew what was bound to come, seized the first chance to give us a warning.

Among the church members at Fort Santiago was L.Z. Villanueva, the son-in-law of Reverend Eusebio Quebral, the Filipino pastor of the Cosmopolitan Student Church. Villanueva had been charged with supplying Mother Stagg with guns, for he was an arms dealer. However, after a month's imprisonment, the enemy released him for insufficient evidence. Before Villanueva left prison, Aqui asked him to pass these words on to the Aquino family: "Ask the dear ones in the hills to clear out" —a warning for us to leave Ipo instantly.

The enemy now knew of the connection Tito and Aqui had with me. They summoned them together, which was unusual. The interrogators questioned Aqui first. Tito saw Aqui beaten several times on the head. Blood gushed forth, streaming down his face and body.

"What are the names and ages of the Chinese newspaperman's children?" the interrogators asked.

"I do not know," Aqui answered truthfully, for he had never learned all their names and ages. For this he was beaten again.

It was a surprise to Aqui that the enemy had centered their attention on our children's names and ages. Someone among the imprisoned church members must have told the enemy about seeing our children at the Aquino house or at the Danses'.

The interrogators now turned to Tito, who, deeply agitated at the sight of Aqui bleeding profusely, gave them a straight answer as he was more familiar with our children. Thus, unwittingly, he revealed that he knew something about my family.

The enemy had obtained what they wanted for that day.

On leaving the investigation room Tito and Aqui were allowed to wash. They rubbed their wounds with salt secretly saved from their meals—a painful but prudent procedure.

"The interrogation will not end here," Aqui whispered. Tito nodded.

Aqui then told Tito of his conversation with Villanueva. "It is our lot. You cannot help but tell the truth," Aqui said. Both thought Villanueva's message had reached us.

Another investigation was called. The enemy now had the case well established. Between blows the interrogators tried to pin Tito down, insisting that if he knew our children he must know my whereabouts. Tito realized that he had been trapped and that there was no way to get out. He begged his captors to finish him once and for all, for he would rather die than break his promise and talk about me.

"No, we will not kill you. We want you to tell us where that Chinese newspaperman is now," the interrogators insisted.

On March 10, 1944, Tito was finally forced to tell a Japanese interpreter of our escape to Ipo.

Tito had suffered much for my sake, and he did not know that the warning for us to leave Ipo had not reached us and that I was still reading and meditating at Camp Hope.

Whether the interpreter was a Japanese, Formosan, or Chinese, Tito could not ascertain. Later, however, we heard that a certain Chinese interpreter had told his family that he had done his part in trying to save Go Puan Seng's life. Just how Tito's answer had been translated we never found out.

# CHAPTER NINETEEN

## A SNAKE-INFESTED LAND

*Man spurns the worm, but pauses*
*ere he wake*
*The slumbering venom of the*
*folded snake.*
Byron: The Corsair I, XI

At suppertime one day Lily, Sister Rosario's niece who had come to stay with us, returned from a visit to the Aquino's road-side house and told us Becky had seen two truckloads of Japanese soldiers speed by their house to Ipo Dam, a few miles east of Aqui's roadside house. The soldiers seemed to be excited. Shortly after, they sped back and went down the hill. We did not give much heed to this report. We thought the Japanese soldiers simply had been making one of their routine inspections of the dam.

Days later, Eddie Marzan said he heard that Japanese soldiers had gone to Tandang Juan's farm. Tandang Juan and his family lived on a hill a few kilometers from Camp Hope on an exposed spot near the highway.

"What happened to Tandang Juan?" I asked.

"Nothing," Eddie answered. Then he added, "The soldiers left after a short while."

As before, we did not pay much attention to this information. Had we known that the two groups of soldiers had been sent after us, we would have been frantic.

The enemy's hunt for us had turned into a drawn-out wild goose chase. After failing to locate us at Ipo Dam, they had tortured Tito again and accused him of lying.

127

Poor Tito! Upon the hammering insistence of the interrogators, he told them how to detour from the highway and get to our hills. However, he deliberately subtracted slightly more than a mile when asked the distance from Manila to the entrance to our trail. Inside the hilly jungle a mile seemed miles. This was his last effort to save us in case we were still in Camp Hope. That was why the soldiers had gone to our neighbor Tandang Juan's place.

Why had the enemy left in such a hurry? Did they consider it unsafe to stay long in the hills? For there were rumors that I had a big guerrilla force with me.

But this was not the end of the enemy man hunt.

We were like the proverbial ostrich burying its head in the sand while its rear is prominently exposed. Soon the enemy was actually to locate Camp Hope. Again, the hour had come.

God in His own Words called us to leave. "Ye have compassed this mountain long enough, turn northward." This Bible verse recurred to my wife's mind in her daily meditation. She pressed me for a decision. "First, the collapse of our chapel; now the call to move from this hill northward; we just cannot ignore these warnings further," she said.

We then related the matter to Yang and Eva. "We do not know what has happened to our good friends inside the enemy's prison. But the situation will not remain static," I emphasized.

"It is always better to be alert," Yang added.

We asked Bayani to look for a new hideout in the hills to the north. "I have no friends in that direction, but I will see," Bayani said. In a few days he had located a two-and-a-half-acre farm in a barrio called Alinsangan. It was a piece of hilly land north of Camp Hope and across the highway. "The farmer who owned the land died of a poisonous snake bite," Bayani reported. "His widow wants to leave the place and has decided to sell it for 1,500 pesos." Anyone would have called it unwise to buy snake-infested land.

The mention of snake-infested land reminded me of a similar place in the Bible. It was the island of Melita. Although the people of Melita were fearful of the venomous reptiles, the

Apostle Paul, armed with faith, was not harmed. It occurred to me that like St. Paul, by trusting in God's mercy, we could set forth to possess the land without fear. With the people around the snake-infested farm avoiding it, it would be an ideal hiding place.

We prayed for assurance.

"Over there is a gleam of sunlight." This message appeared before us as we were guided to open again our daily meditation book, *God Calling*. It meant that darkness would soon pervade the Ipo area, that only over on the hilly land which Bayani had located would there be a small beam of light, and that we should follow it.

To move one step northward across the highway to the new hills did not seem a momentous thing to do, but it was a decision as vital as the one made at the Dans home a year before, when we had left Manila for Camp Hope. Any hesitation then would have involved us in the mass arrest. Any hesitation now could have proved just as fatal.

Eva volunteered to let some of her jewels be sold in the city. A Filipino, she had stood by her Chinese husband through the darkest hours. At first I was reluctant about accepting her offer. I knew how she treasured her jewels. But there was nothing else we could do.

We sent Lily to Manila with the jewels and later received for them exactly 1,500 pesos. Incidentally, our purchase of the hilly land, using Eva's money, was a fulfillment of the guidance received by Yang in March 1943. He had been told to proceed to the hills and to take possession of the land on his second visit just as Caleb had done in the Book of Joshua.

On a moonlit night Yang, Bayani, Fely, and I made our way to this refuge—a rough, rocky area, covered with cogon grass higher than we. There was hardly any level space on which to put up a hut. However, we returned to camp relieved that we had not encountered any snakes.

The deal was closed. We called the land "Mt. Hebron" after Caleb's land.

At first Bayani was enthusiastic. He and Mario started to clear a place to put up a big grass hut for us deeper in the jungle of Mt. Hebron with a small brook nearby. We gave Bayani the money to buy flooring and other boards and transport them to the site. However, before long, Bayani's attitude changed. He thought that, because of Aqui's influence with the neighbors, we could stay in Camp Hope unmolested. In a strange place we would be suspected by the mountain folk around us. He refused to go on with the construction of the hut on Mt. Hebron.

The morale in Camp Hope was evidently on the decline. Mario spent much time visiting Mang Jore, an old farmer who lived with his family about a mile east of Camp Hope. Bayani decided to stay at the Aquino roadside house and come to us only at his convenience. We were helpless.

One day Bayani brought a group of friends to the camp to stay for a few nights. While the strangers were there, we had to confine ourselves inside our hut to avoid detection. I lost my temper; so Bayani stayed away altogether.

We prevailed upon Mario to continue the work at Mt. Hebron alone. Each morning Mario carried his daily ration of rice and salted fish from Camp Hope to our new land, but he took his time doing the job.

The weary days dragged by. Even Yang hesitated about going to this new place when Mario reported that, unlike Camp Hope, Mt. Hebron had no spring.

> I will make them and the places round about my hill
> a blessing; and I will cause the shower to come down
> in his season; there shall be showers of blessing.
>
> Ezekiel 34:26

This beautiful passage which my wife received in her daily Bible reading should have removed our fears of having no water. But just as Caleb's companions were scared by giants they professed to have seen when they first surveyed the land, our companions were reluctant to proceed to Mt. Hebron because of fancied dangers. Very often a person's own inertia is the real giant.

Our lingering too long in Camp Hope could have led to disaster.

Once more God's words came to warn us.

> How long are ye slack to go to possess the land,
> which the Lord God of your father hath given you?
>
> Joshua 18:3

My wife read this Bible verse in her meditation. We had been slow indeed to go in and take possession of the land we had bought. The full impact of our danger struck us only when Lily, whom we had sent to Manila to buy commodities, returned on the night of July 11, bringing with her two copies of the Japanese-controlled *Tribune*. For the first time the case against us was officially disclosed.

The *Tribune* in three successive issues—July 9, 11, and 12, 1944—ran stories about the arrest of priests, nuns, pastors, missionaries, and other persons engaged in underground activities. The enemy's purpose in releasing such publications was to justify the reinternment of the religious workers.

The charges against Mother Stagg were prominently played up.

The enemy called it "The case of one Mary B. Stevens of the Cosmopolitan Church, a Methodist missionary." This was obviously Mary Boyd Stagg since the paper stated that the names were fictitious. "D" was apparently Dr. Darby, while "H," described as working at the Emmanuel Hospital, clearly meant Miss Helen Wilk.

Mother Stagg's case was the first of a dozen published by the Japanese military authorities in the *Tribune*. The number one count against her was that she had helped us to escape knowing full well we were wanted persons. The second count against her was her aid to the Zambales guerrillas under Magsaysay and other groups. The third was her participation in circulating anti-Japanese propaganda prior to December 1943. The top count against Dr. Darby also was the part she had played in sheltering Yang and me. The enemy went further and held her responsible for a loan of 3,500 pesos we had received through Mother Stagg. She was charged with being a third lieutenant and a liaison officer, supplying the guerrillas with ammunition, medicine, and clothing; with circulating anti-Japanese propaganda leaflets; and with exchanging guerrillas' notes for loans from sympathizers. The charges against Miss Wilk were published briefly. We could imagine many more details kept in the Japanese Army files.

These three issues of the *Tribune* reproduced Japanese official documents on underground resistance activities—documents that are glorious historical records of loyal men and women who gave up their lives for freedom.

From the charges against the three missionaries we could conclude that, first, back in March 1942 the enemy had already established a case against us; second, they had been apprehensive over our activities and referred to us as "misguided elements"; and third, they had obtained information about us through interrogations and confessions. We then realized that our movements were no longer secret to the Japanese military authorities and that we could not stay in Camp Hope another day. We decided to move to Mt. Hebron the next morning even though the grass hut had not yet been completed.

Eddie Marzan now began to show his sterling qualities. He left first with our children and Yang's boy Arthur in a careta when the hills were still covered with dew. That same night Lily, Louisa, Fely, and I bade farewell to good old Camp Hope, crossed the highway, and moved to Mt. Hebron. To my surprise and disappointment Yang and Eva changed their minds at the last minute. "Why?" I asked.

"You can go ahead," Yang replied. "Eva and I will stay at Camp Hope for a while with Benny." For the first time since we had been together, Yang had acted against a decision we had both made.

He had apparently believed that the *Tribune* news stories were no cause for alarm. Since the offenses of the three missionaries had now been made public, their cases had undoubtedly been closed. Also, for the past six months the Japanese had not discovered Camp Hope, and probably they never would. These thoughts could have influenced the Yangs to stay on.

Ten days after the rest of us had settled down in Mt. Hebron, the Yangs finally joined us.

One day Eddie returned from a visit with the neighbors. "Some farmers saw a bunch of Japanese soldiers enter the Osboy trail and scout around Camp Hope," he said. "After a while they left the hills." Eddie did not feel any alarm.

It was established later that after the Japanese had failed for the second time to locate us in Ipo, they had put pressure on Tito once more and accused him of fooling them again.

"No," Tito expostulated, "I told you the truth." To Tito the repeated failures of the enemy to locate us were proof that we had left Ipo. Thus, when there was no other way of stopping the beatings, he offered to accompany the Japanese soldiers as a guide. The enemy refused his offer but ordered him to give them a sketch showing how to reach our camp. That was how they had found the Osboy trail. The manhunt had come to its climax. But Camp Hope was now deserted! Had the Yangs delayed further, we could all have been captured.

Looking back on our narrow escape, Yang said, "The ten days we stayed over at Camp Hope, vacillating as to whether to proceed to Mt. Hebron or not, could have cost us our lives. It is during times like this that we know God's power and man's weakness."

# CHAPTER TWENTY

## DEATH BY DECAPITATION

*The sun of those dead heroes has
long since set; but their record
is before me still. And, while the
wind whistles under the caves, I
open my books and read; and lo!
in their presence my heart glows
with a borrowed fire.*

Wen T' ien-hsiang
(1236-1282 A.D.)

Our leaving Camp Hope had saved us from being included in
the mass execution, just as I had escaped death in 1942 when
the enemy wanted to slaughter me along with the Chinese Consul-General and other anti-Japanese leaders.

By the time the charges against American priests, pastors,
and missionaries were made public in the *Tribune,* the fate of
Mother Stagg, Dr. Darby, Miss Wilk, and 31 other heroic men
and women of the Manila Intelligence Group had been sealed.
The mass raid on the church people took place simultaneously
with the enemy's raid on the famed Manila Intelligence Group
and other resistance leaders. The spy who exposed Mother Stagg
was supposed to be the same one who reported the Manila Intelligence Group.

The MIG was headed by Commander Charles "Chick" Parsons, under orders from MacArthur. Chick had been slipping in
and out of the Philippines under the enemy's nose. As a result of
the spy's information, General Vicente Lim, a 1914 West Point
graduate, was captured en route to a rendezvous with Chick

in Mindoro. Captured and later executed together with General Lim were Antonio Escoda, an associate of Roy Bennett of the *Manila Daily Bulletin,* and several other members. General Lim had fought the enemy valiantly in Bataan and had been taken to Capas as a prisoner. Upon his release the general had joined the MIG and defied the enemy to his very end. Chick's own account follows:

> The capture of this group and the torture of a few of the members disclosed the fact that I was awaiting them at Mindoro, which precipitated the dispatch of a punitive patrol to the rendezvous point which almost captured my entire group of about ten people while waiting in the mountains near Paluan. In the surprise raid, Major Philipps was killed and was mistakenly identified by the Japanese as "Chick Parsons" whereupon Tokyo Rose announced in her worldwide broadcast that I had been killed. Major Philipps was buried by the Japanese punitive force at Abra de Ilog, Mindoro, under a headstone with the name of "Chick Parsons."

Major Philipps, Chick's assistant, was the contact through whom Miss Wilk aided the underground.

The enemy, in their early 1944 raids, dealt a heavy blow to the underground activities. But the saga of valor and faith written in blood was even more eloquent inside the prison cells.

Don Juan Miguel Elizalde, a MIG member, was a cellmate of Aqui. During his first month of imprisonment, he was called up for 27 investigations. Each time he was summoned, he would look at Aqui, who would give him an encouraging nod of moral support. Each time he returned, Aqui would rub the raw flesh all over his body with salt they had saved from their meals. "If I ever get out of this cell," Elizalde told Aqui, "I will look after your family." Obviously, he thought Aqui would be killed by the enemy. But it was he himself who became a martyr.

Aqui and Dr. Darby happened to be investigated at the same

time one day. Although they were kept in separate rooms during the investigation, Aqui could overhear the questioning of Dr. Darby because the rooms were separated only by *sawali* (split bamboo) partitions.

"Are you afraid of death?" the interrogator asked with a sneer.

"I believe I have lived my life well, and I am not afraid to die," Dr. Darby answered calmly.

"What would you do if you were allowed to live?" he asked.

"I have been doing the right thing and I should do it all over again," Dr. Darby replied.

Sublime! She lived up to her belief in absolute honesty at the risk of her life. Aqui could not but feel inspired hearing righteousness so bravely upheld.

It was in a prison cell that Aqui met Cardinal Rufino J. Santos. Aqui, a Protestant, and the prelate had been the best of friends. The Cardinal, then secretary to Archbishop Michael O'Doherty, had been arrested and charged with helping guerrillas, distributing propaganda leaflets, and listening to short-wave broadcasts. "If you have faith in God, you will accept all suffering as penance and will not blame anybody for it," he said to Aqui.

After more than a half year of torture and confinement, a general trial was held at the old Bilibid Prison on August 15, 1944. About 90 prisoners were assembled. The sentence was pronounced two weeks later. Thirty men and five women were slain on August 29, 1944. Mother Stagg, Dr. Darby, Miss Wilk, and two other ladies—Mrs. Blanche M. Jurika, mother-in-law of Chick Parsons, and a nun of the Immaculate Conception Convent in Manila—were put to death in the Chinese cemetery —the same place where Consul-General Young and other Chinese leaders had been brutally murdered. Twenty-nine of the thirty men who were executed on August 29, 1944 were identified, and their names appear on the monument over a common grave set up by Don Rafael Roces, now president of the *Philippine Daily Star,* whose son was among the martyred.

The grim possibility voiced by Mother Stagg on her birthday

in 1942 had become a reality: The victims were blindfolded and put to death by decapitation.

> The sun of those dead heroes has long since set; but their record is before me still. And, while the wind whistles under the caves, I open my books and read; and lo! in their presence my heart glows with a borrowed fire.
>
> Wen T'ien-hsiang (1236-1282 A.D.)

Her sister, Mrs. Laura Darby Gray, in response to my inquiry on the life of Hawthorne Darby, wrote the following [January 14, 1966]:

Lafayette, Indiana:

Ever since the time my sister, Hawthorne, was very young, she had already seemed older than her age. It was as though she had the weight of the world on her shoulders—a predestination of her fate. Instead of having fun like most youngsters, she was always very serious. While I spent my money for fancy hair ribbons, sashes, and candies, she would studiously put aside part of the money she earned from helping Mother put buttonholes in the younger children's clothing into her mite box for "Missions."

When Hawthorne went to Depauw University at Greencastle, Indiana, she took a premedical course, for her one great desire was to go to the Philippines and help Dr. Rebecca Parrish, a tiny lady doctor from our small hometown who became the founder of the Mary Johnston Hospital in Manila. However, an uncle of ours, who was a doctor himself, said, "No woman could endure the rigors of medical school." But Hawthorne proved him wrong! She became one of the first seven women ever permitted to enter the University of Pennsylvania Medical School. You should have seen how our family was bursting with pride over her accomplishments on the day of her graduation.

Although the Methodist Hospital in Indianapolis, Indiana, begged her to stay on their staff after her internship with them, she told them that her plans and her destiny were elsewhere.

After spending a summer at the "Ghetto in Chicago" —where she delivered many babies, including a pair of colored twins—up a dark staircase, she spent several weeks in "Lying in Hospital," where the world-famous Dr. Joseph De Lee was the head. Hawthorne was privileged to assist Dr. De Lee on the night Alice Roosevelt Longworth, President Theodore Roosevelt's daughter, gave birth to a baby girl named Paulina. Alice was forty, and this was going to be her first child. When she turned blue under anesthetic, Dr. De Lee turned to Hawthorne saying, "You pray, I think your prayer would do more good than mine." The next day, Alice was saying, "If I had known it was going to be that easy, I would have had one long ago."

In 1925 Hawthorne sailed for Manila in spite of Dr. De Lee's desire to have her on his staff regularly. She worked and lived at Mary Johnston Hospital for several years, delivering thousands of babies.

In 1936 Hawthorne came home for a short visit after having started a successful "Clinic" of her own following her friends' persuasion. When she returned to the Philippines, she took Mother back with her. Then darkening war clouds began to appear, and Hawthorne had to send Mother home with friends.

I now recall that on the morning Hawthorne and Mother left our home in Colfax, Indiana, Hawthorne had said to me, "Remember, Sis, you are next on my list to come to the Philippines." Now this will never be!

# CHAPTER TWENTY-ONE

❦

## OF HEROES AND TRAITORS

*A trusting heart, a yearning eye,*
*Can win their way above;*
*If mountains can be moved by*
*faith,*
*Is there less power in love?*

Frederick W. Faber

A mysterious element in the drama of espionage culminated in the mass execution. The unidentified skeleton among those of the 30 men executed on August 29, 1944 was, according to Chick Parsons, that of one Vero Reyes, who, as Agent Cio, was the man responsible for the capture and execution of the martyrs. So instead of being acclaimed a hero by the enemy he had aided, this spy was executed along with the group against whom he had informed. The kind nature of Mother Stagg, who took the spy into her confidence, was best described in her husband's letter to me written on September 10, 1955, three months before his own death in Palawan, a faraway island down south and off the Sulu Sea.

Samuel Stagg said [September 10, 1955]:

In 1943, I made an abortive effort to rescue her and our younger son, Samboy. I had a rendezvous off Mindoro with a U.S. sub for them. In the effort I lost one guerrilla, had another wounded, and took a bullet in my leg in Culi Culi outside of Manila. I had previously sent word to Mary advising her to stay out of the underground since she would be a marked woman because of Japanese interest in me and I felt that she was too frank and trusting to do that kind of work safely. However, as she was a citizen, she had a right to decide that matter in accordance with her own sense of duty. She was truly one of God's noblewomen.

Mother Stagg, whose maiden name was Mary K. Boyd, was born on April 21, 1893. She and Samuel Wells Stagg were married on Christmas Day of 1917. Stagg came to the Philippines with his family as a young Methodist pastor, and because he was such a brilliant and forceful preacher, he soon gained a great following in Manila. He was later known throughout the Philippines as the "Jungle Philosopher."

Ruth, the Staggs' daughter, had this to say about the early days of her mother's life [January 9, 1966]:

The Boyd family originated in Mississippi. There is a sword that hangs in the Smithsonian Institute in Washington, D.C., which was given to John D. Boyd (Captain in the Revolutionary War) by General George Washington. John D. Boyd was a direct ancestor to my Mother's father who was also named John Boyd. The second John Boyd and his wife, Margaret (called Maggie), moved to California to farm the land. My mother was born in a little hamlet called Lone Star, California. When she was quite young, her father injured his hand and contracted blood poisoning. He was dead within hours and my grandmother was left with five small children, virtually homeless and penniless.

[Ruth went further to describe her mother's character:] My Mother tried to encourage independence in each of us at an early age as a bulwark toward the day when she knew we would be separated. When each child reached his fifth birthday, he was given a letter and streetcar fare and was allowed to go, alone, all the way down town to the Post Office, mail the letter, and return. She encouraged me to have adventures. When I went out to play she would say: "Have an adventure!" Mother was the most fearless, democratic person I have ever known. She was a dynamo of energy. When I was about ten, Mother's spiritual life deepened perceptibly. She got in the habit then of rising in the early hours and having her quiet time with God.

Mother Stagg's missionary work in Manila from 1923 to the day of her death proved her to be a competent leader who was an inspiration to others. It was later revealed by her co-prisoners that even during the time of her imprisonment by the Japanese invaders, when they repeatedly slashed her back and hurt her ailing kidney, she managed to bear everything courageously, singing hymns and reciting Bible verses by heart, just as Paul and Silas had done during their time.

> And when they had laid many stripes upon them they cast them into prison. And at midnight Paul and Silas prayed, and sung praises unto God: And the prisoners heard them.
>
> The Acts 16:23-25

When she knew she had been sentenced to be executed, she was much more resigned to her fate than the others. One of her lady friends, mourning her death, said, "Mary's indomitable will to serve shone clear throughout her whole life. To know Mary is to love her and I know hundreds have said this of her."

Ramon Magsaysay, who became President of the Philippines after the war, thus commended Mary Boyd Stagg: "I knew her very well: In fact I knew not only the part she played in the concerted resistance movement against the aggressor, but also the many beautiful facets of her character. I knew her nobility and courage because there had been more than one occasion when Mary Boyd Stagg, her friends, and I conspired and plotted together against the enemy."

At the time Mother Stagg was sentenced to death, about 60 prisoners in all were sentenced to imprisonment. Aqui's penalty was 8 years, while Tito's was 10, and Samuel Huang's 12. The three were transferred to Muntinglupa Prison.

Ruthless as they were, the enemy failed to put out the flame of resistance. The anti-Japanese movement in the city of Manila had accumulated an enormous number of followers—carromata drivers, laborers, students, educators, politicians, traders, and bankers alike. Underground newspapers edited by men of intellect to counteract enemy propaganda were issued in English, Tagalog, and Chinese. Anti-Japanese and anti-traitor slogans mushroomed everywhere. Handbills were distributed at church meetings and other gatherings.

The enemy might have succeeded at times in cornering these guerrillas, but many a guerrilla would shoot himself before the enemy could lay hands on him. Numerous guerrillas had been executed only to be replaced by new volunteers. Many collaborators met death at the hands of the resistance members. Go Colay, who thought that as president of the enemy-sponsored Philippine-Chinese Association he could be of help to the Chinese, was assassinated. To the patriotic guerrillas cooperation with the enemy meant the weakening of the resistance. Thus his life was not spared.

Less than one short year before, in his attempt to induce me to surrender, Go Colay had thought I would either die of hunger in the mountain fastnesses or be shot by the Japanese. But it was he who could not live through the Japanese occupation. There was risk in battle, in underground activities, and even in capitulation or collaboration. The moment had come for every man to choose good or evil, honor or infamy.

"If I had not left Manila with you, I could have been killed by the enemy during the mass execution or else forced to collaborate only to meet the same fate as the president, vice-president, and secretary of the Japanese-sponsored Philippine-Chinese Association," Yang remarked to me when we received the news of Go Colay's assassination.

I recalled my conversation with Yang and Tony during the

early days of the Japanese occupation. Yang had been right when he foretold that events to come would bring danger not only to me but to all of us.

We had lived through our most perilous period as far as the enemy's manhunt was concerned. But we were to encounter even greater dangers after we had moved from Camp Hope to Mt. Hebron.

# CHAPTER TWENTY-TWO

❧§❧

## THE BATTLE BEGINS

*If you cannot discern the true
shape of Mount Lu,
It is because you are standing
in the midst of the mountain.*
Chinese Poem

The strategic importance of Mt. Hebron was not known to us until we had actually passed through the crisis.

We had come to the Ipo hills and had lived in Camp Hope for 14 months, but we really had very little idea as to the complete picture of the mountains. Apogan Pass, with cliffs and rocks surrounding it, even today serves as a southern gateway to the hilly region. The narrow highway, from south to north, bears toward the east with curve upon curve. Camp Hope was in the southeast sector of Ipo adjoining the Blue Mountains. Mt. Hebron, however, was in the northwest sector, which is composed of two hills. The southeast border of this sector is the highway, and farther to the northwest, beyond the two hills, stood densely wooded smaller hills which ended in the distant Central Luzon plains.

Only a few hills and the highway separated Camp Hope from Mt. Hebron. The distance was short enough to enable us to move everything by foot and by carabao cart, and it was relatively easy for all of us to move from Camp Hope to Mt. Hebron without attracting attention. But it was also far enough to make an enemy hunting party lose the trail, because Camp Hope and the Aquino roadside house were situated in one barrio, called Pinakabalingan, while Mt. Hebron belonged to another, Barrio

Alinsangan. To summarize, Aquino's roadside house, Camp Hope, and Mt. Hebron formed a triangle in a nest of hills.

We started our life in Mt. Hebron at the height of the rainy season. Trees and bushes surrounded our grass house. The jungle of course made a fine screen for us, but at the same time it kept our dwelling place as damp as our hut had been 14 months ago when our families had first arrived at Camp Hope. To settle a large household in a new place is always hard, and it is harder still when the people concerned are fugitives.

Lily and Eddie posed as the heads of the household in this new hilly land. They were our front; they faced the neighborhood people who lived some distance away from us. The two received visitors and returned the visits. Whenever they happened to be out and a neighbor dropped in, Eva would take over. She would apologize for their absence and introduce herself as Lily's cousin. Years of hard experience had made Eva equal to her task. The little girlish fears she might have had were gone, and she carried herself like an old-timer of the hills.

The neighbors had been surprisingly kind to Lily and Eddie. We even had more sources of food around Mt. Hebron than we had had at Camp Hope. There was a mountain trader by the name of Tibong Tagaro who lived near Mt. Hebron and who became a fast friend of Lily and Eddie.

Very few people passed our hills. Since it was a high place, we could see anyone approaching our trail and immediately take cover separately in the bushes or inside the house. Ever since we had moved to Mt. Hebron, the tension seemed to have lessened and we had less contact with the city.

Bayani returned. He would stay with us at times or go to Impo's at the roadside. Though we were in the northwest sector, Mario often went over to the other side of the highway to visit Mang Jore and spend his time. Eddie and Lily had become our mainstays.

We started to improve our living conditions all over again as we had done during the early days of our life in Camp Hope. Eventually we partitioned off three rooms and put up a small annex. The Yangs occupied one room, while the other rooms were occupied by Lily, Louisa, our children, my wife, and me. Our other men settled in the annex.

A nearby brook supplied us with water. We cut a secret passage down the steep slope from the house to the brook—a trail that the women folk used often because of their washing. One afternoon when my wife was about to return from the brook, she saw a multi-colored snake coiled in the way. It must have been poisonous but it did her no harm.

About eleven o'clock one morning, not long after, while most of us were still attending to our chores and only Eva and Benny were left home to watch the hut, Betty crawled back to the house on all fours.

"Why do you look so frightened? And why in the world are you down on all fours?" Eva asked, scared and amused at the same time.

"I was on my way to the brook, bringing more of our dirty clothes to Mama, who is doing the laundry this morning, when I saw a long black snake with its head raised toward me. What's more, I almost stepped on it. I could not shout and neither could I run. My knees gave way, so I crawled back," Betty answered after she found her voice again. Later she told us, "You know, all the time I thought it was following me. But I suppose it was as scared as I was and must have crawled back to its nest."

Every night Yang would tell his boys bedtime stories. Our children would press their ears hard against the grass partition and enjoy his tales of King Arthur and his knights. Before long Andrew called himself Sir Lancelot, while Arthur was Sir Galahad and little Benny, Sir Gawain. The three boys were forever engrossed in sword fights and knightly adventures. I suspected Yang must have added a lot more to make his Arthurian tales last for so many months! The children listened avidly, thrilled beyond words.

Things went on smoothly at Mt. Hebron until little Benny contracted dysentery. He suffered so severely that the Yangs had almost given up hope. Eva, however, prayed throughout the night. Suddenly she heard a voice cry, "Try the lactic acid."

She immediately got up and ransacked the few bottles of

medicine she had brought along. Finding the lactic-acid bottle, which was almost empty, she poured out a teaspoonful. Although the medicine did not look safe because it was old, she gave it to Benny with a prayer.

The next morning found little Benny on the road to recovery. Eva kept thanking God and saying, "If it were peacetime I would never have given Benny Boy the lactic acid, old as it was."

We had moved all our chickens from Camp Hope to Mt. Hebron, but we could only afford to feed them when the children had the luck to find nests of white ants; they thus laid few eggs. My wife reserved each egg for me, except a few spared for Benny.

Before I ate each hard-boiled egg, I would wage a struggle within myself. I wanted to give our children the egg, but I knew I needed it so as to regain my health. I pitied them, but they would be worse off if my physical condition failed. They would gather around me and take turns in licking the shell and I would give them a small bite of the egg white to content themselves.

"I cannot blame you if you think that your father is selfish," I told the children. "I am selfish to deprive you of the food you deserve, but you know Daddy is sick and my survival may mean future happiness for you." The children kept silent. They looked at one another understandingly and smiled.

My wife and Louisa always gave me more rice and corn, at the same time seeing to it that the others had enough. They would eat last, and little. Each grain represented love and loyalty.

One afternoon Bataan, our dog, barked excitedly. We found he had caught a big, long lizard. He had wounded the reptile before it could hurt any of our children. Eddie suggested that we kill the lizard and brew a broth. He and the children shared the broth with the dog. "It tastes like chicken!" Andrew exclaimed.

It was most satisfying to reflect that we were the ones eating a reptile while living on land crawling with poisonous snakes.

On the peak of the hill was a large, flat rock on which I took morning sunbaths. There, in the company only of our faithful Bataan and surrounded by trees and high cogon grass, I read my daily 14 chapters. The Bible took on a far deeper meaning than at any other time, and the more I read, the more interesting it became. Reading the same chapters at different times and under different circumstances, I found various messages suited to each day's need. My coughing stopped. Without medicine and with little nourishment, my health was gradually restored.

Yang and I prayed together every noon, after which we would talk about the war until we would forget the time. Yang, therefore, ate his lunch late. He would not only finish his share of corn and rice but also clean the plates of his two boys, even though there were few grains left over. He became stout and healthy.

We were then in fairly good condition for the coming battle.

Since the early days when I had been confined in the isolation room of Emmanuel Hospital, I had often meditated on the flaming faith of the great prophet Elijah. Suffering from over three years of drought, the people clamored for rain. Elijah prayed. Six times he sent his servant to look at the sky for signs of rain. Six times the servant returned with a negative answer. The seventh time the servant saw a cloud as small as a man's hand. Other people were discouraged, but Elijah knew positively that rain would soon follow.

The enemy occupation had dragged along for nearly three years. To some people liberation still seemed far away. But to us, though the theater of war was far in the distance, each remote battle had a vital part in hastening the enemy's downfall.

Lying on my sun-baked rock at the peak of Mt. Hebron and looking up to the sky, I would imagine that a change in the tide of battle would come as fast as the clouds that rolled by. I would strain my ears, ready to receive any sound which might indicate that American task forces had dropped bombs on enemy installations.

Admiral Chester W. Nimitz's navy had launched the Marianas Campaign. MacArthur's forces were making steady progress in north New Guinea and the Admiralty Islands. Japan sent General Tomoyuki Yamashita, the "Tiger of Malaya," to assume the high command for Philippine defense. Japan had at last realized her failure to win over the Philippine people to her war effort. While the Japanese Army was exerting every possible means to suppress the guerrillas, the Laurel Government was exerting every possible effort to prevent further loss of lives of its own people.

I constantly carried a geography book with me to study the war developments as published in the newspapers. I would analyze the *Tribune* news items from time to time. I knew that the American forces were advancing to the islands of Palau and Yap and the end of the enemy occupation was near. The word "Yap" in Chinese means leaf. It had a special significance for us; I had compared the enemy's war fortune with the rise and fall of the flood during Noah's day. When Noah sent out a dove and it returned with a "freshly plucked olive leaf" in its beak, he knew the flood was almost over.

On a September morning we heard a strange sound, like the drone of many planes approaching. The whole camp gathered to pray, only to find out that it was a swarm of giant bees. It was not what we had hoped, but we were not impatient. On September 21, 1944, Louisa shouted as she pointed at the clouds while stirring the porridge, "Look, many, very many!"

High up in the sky a large number of planes in beautiful formation flew like bees. We knew they were American planes, for the enemy could not have so many. The air squadron came from the Pacific, flew over the Sierra Madre through the Blue Mountains, and then passed our hill and dispersed into smaller groups. One group flew toward Pampanga and its airfield, the former Fort Stotsenburg, now Clark Air Base. Another flew to Corregidor and Bataan. The main group had for its target the enemy installation in Manila. From our hilltop we could see the American Air Force insignia clearly. We waved at the planes and prayed for them. This was the most cheerful day we had had since Pearl Harbor.

Every morning we at Mt. Hebron watched the daily flight of the American air armada heading for enemy installations. On October 20, 1944, our 12th wedding anniversary, we sent Eddie to town for news. For many days we had anticipated an American landing in the Philippines. He returned with no trace of excitement.

"No important news, but I brought along a copy of the *Tribune*," he said as he handed me the tabloid.

I jumped with joy and shouted, "The Americans are landing in Leyte!" The whole camp rushed to me as I read the small news item with the caption: "Squadron of American Warships Entering Leyte Gulf Facing Annihilation." Eddie had taken the enemy's report at face value. One had to find the truth by reading between the lines. I laughed at the Japanese version of this glorious news. Since the American fleet had been able to approach the Philippines and enter Leyte Gulf, it wouldn't be so weak as to face annihilation!

The Japanese had tried to hide the fact that Admiral William F. "Bull" Halsey's Third Fleet had succeeded in destroying the enemy's ships in Philippine waters. Vice Admiral Thomas G. Kincaid's Seventh Fleet, spearheaded by Vice Admiral Marc Mitscher's task force, supported the landing in Leyte. Rear Admiral J.B. Oldendorf's Task Force 77.2 and 77.3 had crushed enemy resistance. Local guerrillas had jubilantly rushed to join the liberation forces and serve as guides and vanguard troops.

It was D-day! MacArthur had returned! At long last we saw the fulfillment of President Roosevelt's Christmas promise way back in 1941—a promise of "powerful help on its way to redeem" us. Our dreams of liberation were not dreams anymore.

On the beach of Leyte, in the air, and on the sea, blood was spilled to free us. The Battle for the Philippines had begun. Many paid with their lives; others lost arms, legs, or eyes. And many throbbing hearts in the Philippines and in the United States across the Pacific Ocean prayed for their dear sons, husbands, and loved ones who were in combat.

Following the American landing in Leyte, the enemy feverishly began to fortify the hills. Explosions could be heard from Apogan Pass, about four miles from Mt. Hebron.

Thrilled because the Japanese were preparing to retreat, I had overlooked the fact that we would soon be caught within the battle zone.

# CHAPTER TWENTY-THREE

## PRAY FOR THE ENEMY

> *Beloved, think it not strange con-*
> *cerning the fiery trial which is to*
> *try you, as though some strange*
> *thing happened unto you.*
>
> Peter 4:12

D-day gave us a new lease on life. The enemy would be busy trying to cope with the American offensive and they wouldn't bother themselves to continue hunting for us anymore. We thought we could sit tight this time inside our hills, waiting for happy days.

At Muntinglupa Aqui believed our hilly region would be safe during the impending Battle of Manila. He told Sister Martha, on her next visit to the prison, to take the family back to Ipo. And so she returned to the hills with Serafin, Jr., Ernesto, Amelia, Priscilla, and the newly married couple—"Baby" (young Martha) and her husband, Chung Ting Wee, a Java Chinese, who had just graduated from the College of Dentistry of the University of the Philippines.

Upon settling down in their roadside house, Sister Martha visited Mt. Hebron with Chung and Baby. Chung had been a good friend to our children when they lived together in the church dormitory. He and Baby agreed to stay at Mt. Hebron.

"The more I observe your hunted life, the more I am convinced God is with you always," Sister Martha said. She went on to explain her inability to warn us after Villanueva had notified her of Aqui's advice for us to clear out. "You need depend on no one. God is taking care of you," she said.

A wonderful Christian! She could have claimed credit for having helped us. She could have blamed our association with her family for bringing misfortune to her husband. But she did not murmur a word against us or the three missionary ladies. She bore her burden with perseverance. Though she was anxious over the fate of her husband, not for a moment did she give up hope that he would be free again.

A few days after Sister Martha's arrival, Sister Rosario made an unexpected trip to Mt. Hebron with Amado. She had come to see Bachy, her only daughter, who was then living with us.

Brokenhearted by Tito's imprisonment, Sister Rosario was emaciated beyond recognition. But suffering as she was, she had kept her faith in God and trusted in our friendship as deeply as ever. Once in a while we sent her niece Lily to the city to purchase commodities, and while there Lily would stay with her aunt. When the American planes had started to raid Manila, Sister Rosario had asked Lily to bring Bachy to Mt. Hebron for safety. She herself had planned to take a small hut near Muntinglupa Prison so that she could visit Tito as often as the prison rules allowed. But she could not stay away long from Bachy.

The added presence of Sister Rosario, Amado, and the Aquinos filled Mt. Hebron with a warm, friendly atmosphere. Everybody rose early and retired late. We united our hearts in daily devotions. Those were the sacred and sweet communions —with the fog covering the hills in the early morning and the flickering flame of a coconut-oil lamp at night—when we unburdened our sorrows to one another and rekindled our hopes and our severely tested faith before the altar of the Lord.

Amado had brought us good tidings this time. My mother had regained her health, and she was to live through all the hazards of war.

Our blessed family fellowship, however, was short-lived.

After being with Bachy for a few days, Sister Rosario began longing for Tito. She proposed to take a trip with Sister Martha to Muntinglupa Prison to visit Tito and Aqui, whose birthday fell in early December. They asked Bayani to accompany them.

Amado, too, planned to leave our hills and go with them to Manila. He had played hide-and-seek during the arrest of the church group. There was no official evidence that the enemy wanted him, but since he was my brother-in-law and had had connections with the missionary ladies, it was possible that he had been watched. Spies were still active in the city. I insisted that he stay in the hills with us until the Americans' return to Manila.

"General Yamashita has thrown his best division into the Battle of Leyte. It is generally believed that it will take months before the Americans can come to Manila," he said.

"In Ormoc alone the fighting lasted almost twenty days," Chung added, taking Amado's side. Ormoc is a city in Leyte Province. "You can imagine how long we still have to wait for the Americans. Even the most optimistic think the earliest will be after April."

This attitude irked me.

"You people from Manila think you know more than we who are hiding in the hills," I said. "Believe me, Yamashita may have been a tiger when he captured Singapore, but he will end up a trapped mouse. He threw his best men into the Battle of Leyte, hoping to stalemate the war. But he has miscalculated the strength of the liberating forces. The more men he sacrifices, the weaker his position will become. He may have waged a twenty-day fight in Ormoc but he cannot keep that up. The Americans have returned; Manila can be liberated any time."

Chung laughed but made no comment. Amado finally agreed with me. That night in our prayer meeting I had a presentiment against the trip to be undertaken by Sister Rosario and Sister Martha, but they had made up their minds to proceed.

Before daybreak Bayani, who was to accompany the two women on the trip, left the roadside house on horseback and took the hilly road near Camp Hope on his way to Mt. Hebron. Suddenly, he was seized by an enemy patrol and thrown into a truck. After the shock wore off, Bayani began to fear that, upon being taken to the enemy's camp, he would be tortured and forced to talk about his activities and this might lead to revealing our whereabouts. The years we had struggled for freedom came to his mind. Should it be taken from us at the moment liberation was in sight?

The army truck traveled at high speed. Bayani, who had not prayed for some time, began to pray in earnest. "God have mercy on my mother," he repeated. He regained his courage and determined to be sacrificed or to escape. He knew every curve of the road. So, at a place where the grass was tall and the highway thickly screened with bushes and vines on either side, he jumped. There was a steep incline off the highway. He rolled to the bottom. The enemy, caught by surprise, brought the truck to a screeching stop several yards down the road. The soldiers aimed their rifles at the moving bushes but, afraid of an ambush, held their fire. The truck soon sped away.

With thorns all over his body and blood oozing from scratches and cuts on his arms and face, Bayani stumbled back to Mt. Hebron, crying: "I have a new life! God made me live again."

We were all astounded. And we were surprised that he mentioned God, for he had seldom joined us in our daily worship. As he recounted his horrible experience, Bayani kept thanking God for His mercy, and we all rejoiced with him.

"God saved you not only physically but spiritually, too. He had brought you back to Him," I remarked. Bayani nodded. It was a narrow escape for Bayani and for all of us as well.

The two women, undaunted, traveled to Manila alone.

After that experience, Bayani was a changed man. Since he now hid with us in Mt. Hebron, he had more opportunity to read the Bible and he joined our meditations on the peak.

One evening Eddie came running. "I saw a large number of Japanese soldiers camping in the nearby hills," he reported. "And Becky said she saw Army Car Number One drive by the Aquino house."

"Army Car Number One?" I asked in surprise. "That's serious. If true, it means Yamashita has come our way." It was evident that the enemy had chosen to take their position in our hilly region. All night long we heard the rumble of heavy trucks on the road below Mt. Hebron. More Japanese soldiers were com-

*154*

ing in, converging in the eastern sector. Heavily armed garrisons began guarding the highway and passersby were held for questioning.

I tried to calm my mind. As usual, I climbed to the peak for my daily meditation and exercise. It was almost noontime. From the top of the hill I saw a lone Japanese soldier armed with a rifle and walking through the farm below our hills and coming in our direction. I jumped into the bushes and hid myself among the thorns and rocks. For a long while nothing happened. When I returned to our house, I discovered that the soldier actually had come up to Mt. Hebron and entered our house. Betty related the event to me:

"The soldier timidly asked Lily to cook the rice he had in his lunch box. While the rice was being cooked, he started to make a paper boat and kept pointing to it and telling us, 'boto, boto.' When it started to shower, he helped us gather the palay [unhusked rice] which was being dried. After the rice was cooked, he asked Lily if there were eggs or vegetables. She gave him some camote tops and mongo. He behaved well and kept saying 'delicious' and 'thank you' while he ate. Before touching his food, he remained silent for a while. I wondered whether he was praying or thinking of his family back home.

"After finishing half of the cooked rice, he stopped. He did not eat more because he had to save the other half for his next meal. He asked for a small package of salt to eat with his rice tonight. How I pitied him! He looked so forlorn and desperate. His shoes were worn out and he wore a rope around his waist for a belt."

Betty went on to tell me that the soldier's knapsack bore two characters, "Shan Sia." In Chinese they mean "beneath the mountain." In Japanese they are pronounced "Yamashita"; hence this young soldier must have been one of the General's guards. This confirmed Becky's report that she had seen Army Car Number One in Ipo.

From Betty's description of the appearance of this soldier, we knew the Imperial Army of Japan was low in supplies. It was understandable that the man felt lonely after years of war in which a host of his brothers, young and innocent, had fought and died on far-flung battlefields from China to the Pacific Islands. And to think of the millions of human lives right then being sacrificed in battle, the many hearts bleeding and weeping.

> O High Heaven! Which of these but has father and mother, who bore them about in childhood, fearing only lest maturity should never come? Which of these but has brothers, dear to them as themselves? Which of these but has a wife, bound by the closest ties?
>
> Li Hua

My late father in his essay on "Opportunity, Force and Sentiment" once said, "Can we rely on Opportunity? Yes, we can, but we must not miss it before it passes us by. Can we rely on Force? Yes, we can, but we must not use it; it recoils against us." I could not help but ponder on how the Japanese had misused their power, and how they had fouled up their whole timetable of the war. They who had attacked others were themselves attacked!

"My child, we hoped for the American forces to come and redeem us, and our hope has become substance. For this young soldier, dark days are just beginning," I told my daughter Betty. "It is rewarding to suffer and hope. It is pitiful to suffer without hope. Having gone through pain and hardships we can sympathize with this desperate young Japanese soldier."

I asked Yang and Betty to kneel with me in prayer. We prayed that the enemy would hasten to concede their defeat so that the war might come to an end and more deaths be prevented.

Before the occupation, I had been a strong advocate of resistance against aggression to the end; now in the midst of fighting, I prayed fervently for peace.

Betty cried as she prayed—this little child who had had to flee from home on her seventh birthday, drifting from place to place with me in my self-exile. Now she was ten, and through suffering in her own life she had come to understand the sufferings of others. For the first time, we were praying not only for our allies, but for the enemy as well—the same enemy who had hunted us for the past three years. The full significance of Christ's forgiveness and love dawned on us.

# CHAPTER TWENTY-FOUR

✦✦✦

## ENCIRCLED

*Jesus said: Peace I leave with you, my peace I give unto you: not as the world giveth, give I unto you.*

John 14:27

The appearance of the young Japanese soldier at Mt. Hebron showed that desperate and hungry enemy troops had begun to forage from house to house in our hilly region.

About dusk one day, a husky young man suddenly came running to Mt. Hebron. It was Ernesto, the second son of the Aquinos. "I have escaped from the Japanese camp in Bigti, a barrio below Apogan Pass," he panted. "Two days ago I was taken near our house by the Japanese soldiers to work on their fortification. I took the first opportunity this afternoon to run away."

Ernesto explained that a large number of people had been forced to work for the Japanese Army and that he should not risk being seen by anyone at the roadside. Accordingly, we asked him to stay with us.

Soon after that incident, Impo and Becky moved with the children to the deserted Camp Hope. Ernesto decided to join them, assuring us that he would be able to dodge the Japanese soldiers inside the jungle. Indeed, this young man was every bit as courageous and tough as his father. We asked Mario to accompany him that night over the trail to Camp Hope.

In the days that followed, the sound of speeding trucks and marching infantry filled the air. We had no way of judging the number of Japanese soldiers pouring into our region, but it seemed they would never stop coming. We woke one morning to see soldiers standing on a neighboring hill. Their camps now stretched from the eastern sector all the way to our vicinity. Desperate soldiers—with guns cocked and bayonets fixed, chasing chickens, ducks, and pigs—became a frightful menace.

Only then did the stark realization come to me that we were in a most precarious position.

I was reading the book of Joshua. The word "westward" came to me time and again. Joshua 16:3 said: "Goeth down westward to the coast." I related this to my wife during our daily meditation. "God guided his people westward across the River Jordan. He is calling us to go west," my wife emphasized.

Beneath and to the west of Mt. Hebron lay the vast central plains of Luzon. I, too, believed God's guidance clearly meant for us to go west and down from the hills to the plains.

" 'Goeth down westward to the coast.' That is Manila," Yang casually interpreted when I told him about the Bible verse. (Manila, the capital city, is situated along the coastal area.) Although in the ensuing days we were to go first westward and then down south to the coast—to the city of Manila, which had been the object of our prayers for the past three years—at the time, we made no plans to move.

With the tense situation grown worse, I called our men to an emergency meeting at the peak and analyzed the situation to them. "The enemy is running to the mountains to keep away from the Americans. He is fortifying this rocky region. And we are inside the battle-line!" This conjecture proved right. It was known later that General Yamashita had put up his first line of defense in the Ipo region to cover his retreat to Baguio, Mountain Province, far to the north of us. Only the 26th Division of Major General Shizue Oki was left to stick it out in Manila and its northeast suburb of Marikina Valley.

Considering our situation, Yang was worried but made no suggestion. Eddie listened intently while Chung maintained his usual attitude of indifference. Bayani complained that it was my fault for objecting to his bringing strangers to Camp Hope. Those strangers had farms deep in the Blue Mountains. "If we had been friendly to them, we could have escaped to them now," he said. Mario also spoke up. He proposed we move back to Camp Hope. He believed that there we could count on the help of Mang Jore, a kindly farmer who was generally respected. And from there we might easily move deeper into the Blue Mountains.

The highway between Camp Hope and Mt. Hebron was alive with Japanese soldiers retreating from the plains. The Blue Mountains were more accessible from Camp Hope, and the plains from Mt. Hebron. If we proceeded to the plains, we would be traveling toward the retreating Japanese soldiers and exposing ourselves to possible encounter with them; while if we crossed the highway, retraced our steps to Camp Hope, and then continued deeper into the mountains, we would be running ahead of the incoming soldiers and maintaining a safe distance between us and them. In this way we could avoid coming face to face with them.

It was natural for the men around me to insist that we withdraw to the Blue Mountains. I, also, thought that to risk facing the Japanese soldiers would be most dangerous. Not only had many people been conscripted, but some had been killed in cold blood when encountered by the enemy.

During the last three years there had been many crises requiring vital decisions in which we had subjected our own reasoning to God's guidance. I brought up this point at the meeting.

"We are facing the severest test of all at this time," I said. "Bayani's and Mario's reasoning is sound. But we were guided to come to Mt. Hebron and had been warned that only over here would there be a gleam of light for us to follow. Shall we now act contrary to God's Guidance and turn back in the direction of Camp Hope?"

They all kept quiet.

The meeting adjourned without a decision being reached. We drew closer to God in the long quiet hours that night. My wife and I became stronger in our belief that we should not turn back to Camp Hope.

As the cock crowed, I called Yang. I explained to him that the strategic hilly region of Ipo had been "darkened" by the infiltration of large numbers of retreating Japanese soldiers. Our flight northward from Camp Hope to Mt. Hebron was meant as the first step to get us out of the mountains and down to the sunny plains.

"When the enemy took to the plains, we took to the hills; now that the enemy is taking to the hills, we shall take to the plains," I said. "We must proceed forward, to the plain, not backward to the Blue Mountains. We have no idea how to avoid a face-to-face encounter with the inpouring Japanese from the plains, but we must simply remain steadfast in the Divine Guidance, trusting God to open the way for us."

Yang and Eva shared our belief.

We gathered the members of the clan and told them of the decision. Bayani was silent. Mariu left for Camp Hope to join Mang Jore.

Despite the confusion, our womenfolk had the presence of. mind to slaughter the livestock for food so as to lessen our burden when we should commence our coming flight. There also was the possibility of our wandering pigs, cows, and chickens luring soldiers to our hiding place.

The women decided to butcher our pig first. Unused to the grisly task, they spent a whole morning trying to slaughter it. By the time the men came home for lunch, the poor stuck pig was still squealing with a hoarse voice. The women had already started to scrape off its hair.

Next we decided to butcher the cow. Just as Bayani was about to hit the cow with an ax, he saw tears streaming from its eyes. He couldn't bear to continue. The children, torn between the desire to say good-bye to their cow and the fear of watching the slaughter, ran into our room and peeped through holes. We finally had to cover the cow's head with a piece of black cloth before dealing the final blow. Our boys and girls came out of the room weeping. But they, too, enjoyed the beef broth later, which they had not tasted for so long. Having to shed the blood of our pets was a nightmare, but we had to face reality. The salted pork and beef tided us over for quite some time.

We were finally packed and ready to leave Mt. Hebron. God had opened the way. We were to cut a path of escape through the densely wooded smaller hills beyond Mt. Hebron. And the instrument was the young and inexperienced boy, Eddie Marzan, who had been thrust upon us by Aqui against our wishes.

Eddie, through his good friend Tibong, the mountain trader, had come to know Mang Genio Tagaro, Tibong's elder brother. The Tagaros lived on a farm to the northwest below our hills. It was on the edge of the hilly sector, a step closer to the plains. After listening to me at our recent conference when I had talked in favor of heading for the plains, Eddie took the initiative and discussed our problem with his new friend, Mang Genio. This simple farmer immediately offered us his house. The Japanese soldiers had not penetrated to his area.

Eddie, however, kept his conversation with Mang Genio to himself until we had gathered one night to plan seriously for our new move. "Mang Genio's place will be a stepping-stone to the plains. I think it offers the best way out so far," Eddie concluded.

I was perturbed that he had confided in a stranger.

"Facing our situation squarely, it seems to me that Eddie's proposal is the only way," Yang remarked. "We've got to be sensible."

We had long prayers together. We finally asked Eddie to arrange a meeting between Mang Genio and Yang. Yang could speak the native dialect and had always displayed tact in dealing with strangers. He was impressed by the farmer's willingness to help. He believed Mang Genio commanded the respect of his neighbors, near and far, just as Mang Juan had in his community.

Arrangements were made with Mang Genio for us to start moving to his farm on Christmas night. We wished to observe our Lord's birthday at Mt. Hebron, regardless of the grave situation.

At eventide Eddie, Amado, and Chung played the roles of the Three Wise Men from the East. Cloaked in bathrobes, blankets, and pajamas, and holding a pot, a plate, and a piece of soap as gifts, they paraded solemnly before us all. What a comic picture they made! With the threat of death over us, we had, nevertheless, a blessed Christmas behind the Yamashita Line enjoying "the peace that passeth all understanding."

> Jesus said: Peace I leave with you, my peace I give unto you: not as the world giveth, give I unto you.
>
> John 14:27

After our Christmas celebration, the Yangs, the Chungs, and Bayani moved from Mt. Hebron to Mang Genio's, but we stayed behind overnight because we wanted to celebrate Andrew's birthday also at Mt. Hebron. Our boy had come to us two hours after Christmas five years before.

The children were always cheerful, for they had become used to poverty and danger. The next morning—after singing "Happy Birthday" to Andrew—three of our girls, Elsie, Cecilie, and Betty, accompanied by Eddie, hiked to Mang Genio's. Bachy, Dorcie, and Andrew were to leave with us that night. I was reluctant to say farewell to Mt. Hebron, for here I had regained my health and here we had first seen the war planes of the liberation forces. Mt. Hebron had been a promise and a gift.

Our lingering at Mt. Hebron for another day enabled Sisters Rosario and Martha to see us. They had returned to find the peaceful hilly region now a war-torn area. They had come over the hills, risking capture by the Japanese soldiers. No danger was too great for the tender hearts of these mothers. Sister Martha hurried to Camp Hope to join the rest of her family and promised to see us at Mang Genio's.

Thankful that she had arrived in time, Sister Rosario lifted Bachy in her arms and left Mt. Hebron with the rest of us that night.

Eddie had returned to escort us. "The Yangs, the Chungs, and all the children have settled at the new place nicely," Eddie said. "Mang Genio will come halfway from his house to meet us beneath our hills." Eddie's report lightened our hearts. Courageous young Lily was left behind for a night and was to leave early the following morning with the rest of our belongings. Eddie was to return to Mt. Hebron after escorting us.

We were again on the run, this time seeking shelter in the home of a complete stranger. The moon was not shining but a few stars guided us along our path. Step by step, we cautiously moved on until at last we saw a carabao-drawn cart coming toward us. It was driven by Mang Genio, a short and stocky farmer over thirty years old. He was calm and spoke little, but he immediately attended to our belongings, which we loaded on the careton. We hiked over another hill before reaching his place an hour later. Banana plants fenced his camote plantation. In the center stood his big wooden house, which he offered to us. He moved his wife, his boy Pedring, and his three daughters—Erene, Sotera, and Apolonia—to a smaller storehouse near the trail. He had another boy, Pelagio, who was visiting his in-laws at Tigbi, a neighboring barrio.

That night we enjoyed peace at Mang Genio's, free from the yells of the enemy.

The quiet was broken early in the morning, however, by the excited voices of Lily and Eddie. Japanese soldiers had invaded Mt. Hebron at daybreak. The officers had immediately headed for the peak, my "Upper Room," where I had held my morning meditation. "The soldiers looked around and ordered us to move out at once," Eddie said. Lily chimed in gleefully that they had managed to smuggle out our four chickens.

# CHAPTER TWENTY-FIVE

❦❦❦

## THE INNER STRUGGLE

> *O send out thy light and thy truth:*
> *let them lead me. . . .*
>
> Psalm 43:3

Once again we had eluded the Japanese soldiers in the nick of time. "God will never forsake you," Mang Genio said many times. Eddie told us later that Mang Genio had suspected we were some persons the Japanese wanted; being a guerrilla himself, he was willing to risk helping us. We bought camotes, rice, eggs, and chickens from him and his wife.

By then our finances had reached rock bottom. Lily volunteered to secure funds from our friends in Manila. She had been asked by her aunt to accompany her to the city. Sister Rosario had decided to leave Bachy and visit Tito once more. Little did she know what dangers her only daughter would have to go through with us!

After Sister Rosario and Lily left, there was a short spell of quietness in which we got better acquainted with Mang Genio's family. One morning Mang Genio, with a rifle strapped over his shoulder, came to our house showing us a cigarette package bearing MacArthur's "I shall return" message on the wrapper. "Guerrillas visit me often. They are my friends. There is no fear of trouble," he said proudly. He stowed away the precious package and his rifle in the house we were occupying.

Though we all were living in a twilight zone between life and death, the few days that we had been at Mang Genio's confirmed our belief that his farm was a safer place than Camp Hope.

"Could you get a house nearby for our friends, the Aquinos?" I asked Mang Genio.

"Yes, I can get one," he replied. "The neighbors are all my friends. They are most accommodating folks."

Yang shared my desire to invite Sister Martha and the rest of her family to join us. We sent Eddie to slip through secret mountain trails and convey our message to them.

"They cannot make up their minds and prefer to wait a little while to watch the outcome." We were all disappointed when Eddie said this upon his return.

Accompanied by Mang Genio's son Pedring, Baby courageously risked a trip to Camp Hope and brought back her brother, Serafin, Jr., whom we called "Boy." Just how Baby convinced her mother to allow her brother to come, she did not explain. What we knew was the fact that though Sister Martha shrank from deciding an issue that would determine the fate of her entire group, she was willing to allow her sixteen-year-old son Boy to join us.

"We have found a house for you," I was glad to tell Sister Martha when she surprisingly came with Becky the following day. At first I thought her group had finally decided to accept our invitation to join us, but was disappointed to find out that she came with Becky only for a short visit with us and to talk to Boy and Baby. I told her it would be better for us all to abide by God's guidance and struggle together.

She listened to me eagerly but made no commitment. "I will discuss the matter further with the folks," she replied, dismissing the subject politely.

Before she left with Becky, she promised to return and see us again. It was New Year's Eve. They were in a hurry to join their family at Camp Hope.

That night we held a prayer meeting as usual and drew promises from the Bible in the wee hours. I received this passage.

For the mountains shall depart, and the hills be removed; but my kindness shall not depart from thee,

neither shall the covenant of my peace be removed,
saith the Lord that hath mercy on thee.

Isaiah 54:10

At that moment little did I realize how literal this passage was going to be. The ensuing fight waged in Ipo left the hills barren and the mountains bald. Everything was razed by the intensive bombings that followed.

We knew we were up against further dangers.

A week later Sister Martha came back, this time with Gorgonia, her maid. Avoiding the sentry lines at the highway, they smuggled in a leg of goat with them. They had butchered their timid little goat and wanted us to have some of the meat. But that was not all. She had come to offer to share their rice with us. Instead of being persuaded to come to us, she urged us to go back to Camp Hope.

"According to reports," she said, "a big battle is expected to be fought in your area. I talked to Mang Jore about you. He's willing to help. He assured me he would do his best to see us all safely through this war. We still have fifteen sacks of palay. If worse comes to worst, we can depend on that to tide us over. We can also move into the Blue Mountains. You must join us while there is still time."

She went on to explain that it would be hard for them to come to our place with the palay, which they had hidden inside the bushes near Mang Jore's. The Japanese soldiers had been searching avidly for food and contraband and would confiscate the rice when they saw it.

If the Americans should attack the enemy in Ipo, from the plains and from the northwest, the impending battle would surely begin in our sector for we were right in their path. This had decided Sister Martha and her group to stay on the eastern side.

I was silent for a long while.

The vital issue of returning to Camp Hope again reared its head. On me fell the task of deciding whether to go back east-

*167*

ward with Sister Martha to get farther away from the firing lines and rely on the help of Mang Jore and the security represented by 15 sacks of rice, or to stand firm in God's Guidance and stay in our sector with the hope of being able to move westward to the plains.

Lily had not yet returned. She might have been captured on the way to Manila; even if she had reached the city safely, would she be able to get what we needed and slip through the sentry lines again on the way back? With a troubled heart I asked Sister Martha to pray with us. It was our last prayer together.

My faith resurged. My weak moment was over.

"Sister, I appreciate your kindness very much, but I firmly believe we should follow God's Guidance," I told Sister Martha. It was difficult for me to say it, but there was no alternative.

Since she feared that our sector would become the first battlefield and since we did not know what means of survival we would find if Lily failed to return, I could not be too insistent that she and her group come and join us. Oh, the folly of my little faith!

"What about Boy, Baby, and Chung? We are willing to keep them with us, but if you believe they will be safer with you, we shall abide by your decision," I said.

"I know God is with you," she answered without hesitation. "I shall leave them in your care." Poor, good woman! She was willing to abide by faith for her son and daughter.

In parting I said, "Sister, all of us are living by moments in this terrible emergency. The situation keeps changing, and we do not know when we shall be able to contact each other. We do not know when and where our next move will be and may not be able to inform you. They are your children."

She replied, "Whatever your next decision will be, Boy, Baby, and Chung will follow you. You need not inform me."

Before she left, she talked for a long time with Serafin, Jr. "Boy," she said, "you must behave like a man and do away with your stubbornness and be courageous always." It seemed to Boy as if she were giving her last words to him. He watched his mother leave. Time and again she turned back and waved her hand to him until she disappeared into the jungle.

## CHAPTER TWENTY-SIX

## THE LAST RAID

> *Yea, the sparrow hath found an house, and the swallow a nest for herself, where she may lay her young, even thine altars, O Lord of hosts, my King and my God.*
> Psalm 84:3

Sister Martha had left us a day too soon, for Lily arrived the next morning.

We heard Lily crying as she approached. We were shocked. "What happened? Don't cry. As long as you have arrived safely, we are grateful," my wife said, putting her arms around her. Shaken by sobs, she related how the Japanese soldiers had taken away from her the canned goods and sugar cakes she had brought for the children. Otherwise, she had been unmolested. With one hand wiping away her tears, she reached inside her blouse with the other and handed us a small package of prewar Philippine currency, "genuine money." We all smiled with relief.

"Lily, you are a most courageous girl. You have accomplished a very important mission. We have every reason to be thankful," I told her. She had followed our instructions to contact Pastor Chua for a loan of prewar Philippine currency. She had secretly presented him with a note in my wife's handwriting together with my wife's wristwatch. The note and the wristwatch, easily recognized by intimate friends, proved beyond all doubt that Lily was no imposter or spy.

Through the pastor, our friends in the city ran a great risk in complying with our request for the loan. They were not only aiding hostile elements but sending us prewar currency, which had been declared illegal by the Japanese Army. We had anticipated that when the Americans landed in Luzon, transactions would have to be made in genuine, prewar money.

Lily had brought with her a few copies of the *Tribune*. There was an extra with screaming headlines which claimed that many American planes had been shot down over Formosa. I tried to construct the true picture from the Japanese version. I said to Yang, Chung, Amado, and the others, "From these Japanese claims, we can surmise that the American air attack on the Japanese bases at Formosa, north of Luzon, was very heavy. This attack of the Americans could be the prelude to a Luzon landing. It won't surprise me if MacArthur lands at Lingayen Gulf and strikes at Manila, using the same route the Japanese once used. From now on, let us train our ears for the sound of guns to the west."

They all laughed.

We did not anticipate that on that very night the Japanese troops would extend their lines near us.

The next morning, when we were having breakfast, a group of Japanese soldiers, composed of a captain and several privates, suddenly came to raid Mang Genio's place. One of them, who was extremely ugly, was later described by the children as "monkey face."

The soldiers did not know our identity. They started to search for money and contraband and began with the quarters opposite ours which were occupied by Baby and Chung—he being the neatest and most dignified looking because of his spectacles and bald head. The soldiers went through his belongings thoroughly, intrigued by his watch and camera and especially by his amusing piggy bank. They questioned him and wound up by confiscating the bank, which contained his last savings. Boy served as the interpreter because the soldiers could speak neither English nor Tagalog, the Filipino language. Boy and his brother had continued their schooling during the early part of the occupation and had learned some Japanese.

Our ever-smiling Chung, with his disarming, indifferent air, served a very important purpose. He was like a seemingly expendable pawn in a chess game which suddenly becomes a vital factor in determining the winner. How calmly he and his wife faced the Japanese raiding party, not showing the least trace of fear in their faces! The soldiers took Chung as captain of the house.

The Japanese search of Chung's quarters took a long time. Seeing that the raiders were about to search our quarters, Lily approached me. "Uncle," she whispered as I sat in a remote corner, "where is your manuscript?" She knew it would mean massacre if it were discovered.

"With the blankets here," I whispered back. Lily's face turned pale.

My manuscript, mostly in Chinese, could have been easily understood by the soldiers. It had been left behind at the Dans home, where it had escaped the enemy's search, and later smuggled to Ipo by Lily on one of her trips from the city. It had since accompanied me wherever I went as I took random notes now and then, and it was now kept in our corner. Mang Genio's one-room house did not have any partitions. So the Yangs, the Chungs, my family, and the rest of our group each occupied a part of the floor. When the soldiers entered, my wife had pushed the manuscript under the children's pillows and blankets. There was no possibility of slipping it outside.

We kept the genuine money which Lily had brought back with her inside a native rattan suitcase, which my wife sat on throughout the search. And Mang Genio's rifle and cigarette wrapper bearing the inscription of MacArthur's "I shall return" were in the rafters over another corner.

Yang, the ever-alert, picked up a bunch of bananas and offered one to each soldier in turn, saying "nana, nana," until he got through the guard at the door. He sneaked out unnoticed and headed for the forest to seek refuge. While he was offering the bananas to the soldiers, he kept glancing at me. I knew what was in his mind, but being stout and clumsy, I could not move as fast as he. Any attempt on my part to escape with Yang would only have invited the soldiers' suspicion. If a massacre had taken place that day, after three years and seven days of exile, Yang would probably have been the only survivor.

"Thy will be done, Lord," I kept repeating quietly. I could not say a long prayer.

*Let but my fainting heart be blest,*
*With thy good Spirit for its guest,*
*My God, to thee I leave the rest;*
*Thy will be done!*

Charlotte Elliott
1789-1871

My hair was long and I had not shaved for days. The leather coat I wore was threadbare. Amado was sitting on the floor beside me. The soldier merely threw me a casual glance and went on to question the others.

Suddenly a zooming sound overhead attracted the soldiers' attention. For the first time American fighters appeared over our sector. Four American planes were flying very low. Monkey Face pulled out his pistol, rushed to the window, and aimed at a plane. A single shot could have invited machine-gun fire from the air. We would have been certain victims—killed either by the desperate Japanese soldiers or by the bullets of the American planes. But I was too excited then to think of the danger. I interpreted the unexpected presence of the American planes as God's answer to our prayers.

The Japanese captain had the presence of mind to pull Monkey Face down and order everyone to lie flat on the floor and keep silent. When the planes zoomed away, the soldiers' arrogance went with them. They knew that they had to leave soon for safety. Hurriedly they picked up a few things only to throw them down again.

"What is this?" A soldier touched the pillows and blankets in our corner.

"Children's pillows and blankets" Boy translated for my wife.

"Ah!" the soldier nodded. He did not uncover anything.

Mang Genio's rifle, the cigarette wrapper, and the money had also escaped their search. "We're coming back," the soldiers told us.

As soon as they had left, Lily pulled out my manuscript. She wrapped it in the old canvas bag which my wife had given me on December 31, 1941, when I had left home with Tony and Yang, and stowed it in a kerosene can. She hid this in a ravine among the bushes beside a brook. Mang Genio got his rifle and cigarette wrapper and buried them in the forest.

We men spread out in the jungle, fearing Japanese soldiers might surprise us again and recruit us for forced labor. We planned to return after dark.

I climbed among some rocks and sat between two huge stones. The sound of heavy boots tramping came from all directions. Alone in the jungle, I worried over what might happen to our women and children. I experienced the same anxiety I had felt when Dominador had warned me of the manhunt early in 1942. I prayed. This time not Psalm 27 but Psalm 37 sustained me:

> Fret not thyself because of evildoers, neither be thou
> envious against the workers of iniquity. For they shall
> be cut down like the grass, and wither as the green
> herb.
>
> Psalm 37:1, 2

It was the opening verse of the Psalm and foretold the flight of the enemy. The Psalm went on to promise security to those who would take refuge in God.

As the day slowly neared its end, I came down from the rocks. I had spent far more time in meditation than I had planned. The jungle darkness began to close in on me. I was lost. I stumbled over fallen tree trunks, clinging vines, rocks, and anthills as I groped my way through the forest.

When all the other men had returned, my wife and Yang began to worry about me, fearing I might have been taken by the enemy. The whole household was aroused. Mang Genio, Lily, and Yang set out with a lamp in an attempt to find me.

I slipped and fell. The next minute I sat up and saw Yang with a lamp. We had met in Mang Genio's camote field.

Entering the house, I was happy that everybody was safe. As our children gathered around me to pick the thorns out of my clothes, my wife wept.

"Don't cry," I said. "It's good to be back."

# CHAPTER TWENTY-SEVEN

❦

## THROUGH YAMASHITA'S LINE

> *I waited patiently for the Lord;*
> *and he inclined unto me and*
> *heard my cry.*
> *He brought me up also out of*
> *an horrible pit, out of the miry*
> *clay and set my foot upon a rock,*
> *and established my goings.*
>
> Psalm 40:1-2

The raid had awakened us to the urgent need of leaving Mang Genio's place. Bombs fell on Norzagaray, a nearby town. Loud explosions issued from the northwest and fires shot sky-high. The Americans had begun their air attack on the hilly region after they had spotted the Japanese concentration points.

"We must be on the run," I told my companions.

But there was hardly a breach in the Japanese cordon for us to sneak through. That night we sent for Mang Genio for an immediate conference. Yang tried to persuade him to evacuate the area, but he did not want to leave his home.

"I heard that people caught trying to get out of the hilly region have been killed," Mang Genio said. "We'd better stay here for the time being." Of course his view was well taken, for unless we could be sure of finding a safer place, there was no sense in risking encounters with the enemy. But to stay within the firing line was a sure way to meet death. Before Mang Genio went back to his storehouse, I said to him, "We shall pray that God will guide you to lead us to a safer place at the right time." He made no comment.

175

A moment later the time came! His brother-in-law, Mang Sabino, arrived unexpectedly to ask Genio and his family to move to his own home at Barrio Tigbi. Mang Sabino had heard the rumor that our sector would soon become a battlefield, and he had lost no time in urging Genio to hurry. Genio was now convinced of the gravity of the situation and decided to move his family out with us. Mang Tuya, a guerrilla lieutenant who was the husband of Genio's sister and who lived nearby, decided to bring his family and join the exodus. Genio returned to the big house and told us of Sabino's proposition.

"Sabino said he did not meet any Japanese soldier on the way from his home to Alinsangan," Genio reported. "It seems to me that we can go to Tigbi."

"Where is Tigbi?" I asked.

"It is out of our hilly region and down at the plains," Genio replied. A small and seemingly isolated barrio, Tigbi stands some distance west of Genio's farm. The direction coincided with the Bible verse, "Goeth down westward to the coast." The Divine Guidance was approaching its full realization although we were not completely aware of it until later.

"Can we start now?" I asked again.

"We can start any time you wish," Genio replied in the casual, phlegmatic manner of the mountain folk.

We were about to undertake a most dangerous journey. The Japanese troops were constantly moving. Any moment the situation might change. The way by which Sabino had traveled was passable today but might not be so tomorrow. Getting our whole group safely out of the enemy encirclement seemed as hard as extricating oneself from a trap. We gathered that night, calling upon God to give us words of assurance on this vital move. We placed our full trust in Him and we were guided again to open *God Calling*. These words appeared: "Rise from death to life." It would be death this time if we refused to heed the warning. I asked everyone to pack and stand by.

God had told us to rise, to take immediate action, but we were still held back by our human inertia and fear of the unknown. We prepared to move, but we did not start moving. Early next morning Yang, Bayani, and I went to the jungle to discuss the situation. Lily ran to us breathlessly. "A big group of Japanese soldiers has surrounded the house and ordered our people to leave," she said. The soldiers were Formosans and comparatively well-behaved. They talked to our women politely and confirmed the rumor that Ipo would soon become a battlefield. The sooner we left, the better.

"Auntie Fely and Auntie Eva have already moved out some of our things," Lily continued. "They ask that you come back to the house immediately."

I felt no panic this time. Instead, I thought of the arrival of the Formosan soldiers as a blessing in disguise, for it forced us to move and allowed no more time for hesitation.

As we approached the house, we were surprised to see young Formosan soldiers helping our women carry the younger children down the bamboo ladder. They did not know who we were, and we could feel no animosity toward them—only appreciation for their helpfulness.

Several American B-24's suddenly roared above us. The soldiers took cover. This gave us time to pack a few more belongings. Every little thing was so precious that it was hard to decide which was most important. I stood outside, admiring the American planes, which flew very low in beautiful formation. I trusted that the American pilots would see we were civilians and would not drop any bomb.

We had delayed too long; we had failed to grasp the fact that other detachments of soldiers would follow the Formosans and might not be so kind. It was foolish also to believe that the American planes were flying above the battle lines merely to stage a spectacular display.

Bayani was alert this time. "Uncle, God has opened the way for us and we must not waste any time. The soldiers might change their minds any moment," Bayani whispered to me.

Abruptly, I asked Yang and Chung and the women to leave behind all that was unpacked and to start immediately. How right Bayani was! Barely two hours later another group of Japanese soldiers arrived at Alinsangan and prohibited the remaining civilians from leaving the area.

Carrying our belongings, we set out single file. The heavier things were fastened to bamboo poles and carried on our shoulders. Louisa had to carry our blankets and pillows. Eva carried Benny. My wife carried Bachy, the Danses' little daughter, on one arm and a big basket on the other. Our boy, Andrew, was helped by Amado and walked by himself at times. We did not use our careta so that Boy Aquino could ride on the carabao's back, for he was not well.

Poor Bachy. We had watched her grow from infancy. With her father in enemy hands and her mother's fate unknown, she might have to face the future by herself. As for Boy, his mother, brother, and sisters had gone the other way. He and his sister Baby were left to look for their father, if the enemy ever released him.

Bataan, our faithful dog, used to staying behind each time we moved to a new place, failed to follow us. We could not call him by name for fear the soldiers would become suspicious. He must have fallen into the enemy's hands, as did Bataan Peninsula three years before.

With Bayani leading the way, we stepped into the wilderness again under the open sky. The wind from the north blew cold and heavy. Passing clouds covered the sun every now and then. None could tell what lay ahead.

So Hsuan, an ancient Chinese scholar, once said of the ideal general:

> With a huge mountain collapsing before him, the color of his face should remain unchanged. With deer jumping at his side, his eyelids should not even tremble.

Courage and firmness were the qualities that made a great general. Being in the battle zone behind the Yamashita Line, we had to be just as firm in our faith.

On and on we went, till at last we came to a river. Glancing toward it, we received a jolt. There, in the water, Japanese soldiers were bathing! They were trying pathetically to wash the itches and boils that covered their bodies. Seeing our group, some soldiers came toward us. Bayani's face took on the same pallor it had shown when he had escaped from the Japanese truck and had run to Mt. Hebron. Our hearts started throbbing. A Japanese soldier grabbed Boy and wrested from him his camera. It was no use for Boy to resist. Another one tried to open a jar of olives Dorcie was carrying. We had kept this jar for three years. Dorcie innocently and stubbornly held the jar tight and turned away. The soldier laughed and left the children alone. We kept silent, but I knew everybody was praying. Slowly and fearfully, we forded the river.

Bayani, in his haste, had led us the wrong way. All the time we had been following the regular trail, which was infested with Japanese soldiers! Mang Genio now caught up with us and told us to detour immediately. We began to hike across deserted field, through thick forests and brooks, through vines and thorns.

"Beware, quicksand!" someone shouted.

We stopped as we saw something moving a few yards away. It was a horse frantically struggling to free its feet from a big pool of sand. The harder it tried to get out, the deeper it sank until it was finally engulfed. This was our first encounter with quicksand. We had never imagined how horrible it could be!

We detoured again. Up and down one hill after another, we zigzagged along, through farmyards and over fences. The farmers knew Mang Genio. Many of them were surprised to see us. We did not follow the mountain trails but hewed our own path.

From morning till noon we kept on. The hot, tropic sun parched our throats. Louisa, who could not endure her thirst, drank stagnant rain water from a hole in a ravine. Some of the children followed her example.

At the foot of a hill we came to another farmhouse. Several people had gathered there to discuss the latest grapevine news: MacArthur's forces had landed at Lingayen!

I looked at Amado and Chung who looked back at me with approving eyes as they remembered my prediction. The glad tidings of liberation were like a shot in the arm for us weary refugees. It was January 9, 1945. Admiral Daniel E. Barbey, under Admiral Kincaid's command and in coordination with reinforcements from Admiral Theodore S. Wilkinson and Richard L. Connolly, had successfully landed the liberation forces at San Fabian, Pangasinan Province, 141 miles north of Manila.

Squadron after squadron, the American airplanes swept back and forth across the sky. Step by step, we progressed from hill to hill. We were walking in the shadow of death.

After eight hours of our barefoot hike, the sun was sinking, with only a gleam left to guide us as we passed through the Yamashita Line and entered the little village of Tigbi. It was the first time our children had stepped on level ground for months. They had been used to the feel of stones and grass under their feet, and they felt uneasy and strange walking on the smooth road. Mang Genio's father and mother-in-law, and all their relatives, welcomed us with traditional hospitality.

Eight hours' hike was not a long journey, but a distance of eight hours had taken us out from the hell of a horrible battlefield.

"Are any Japanese soldiers posted here?" I asked Mang Genio, who had been gathering information from our hosts.

"No," he answered.

"Have any Japanese soldiers ever passed through this village?" Yang inquired.

"Not one," was the reply.

Tigbi was an unimportant and secluded little village. We could not be sure of absolute security anywhere, but we knew that here on the plains our lives were safer. And then American war planes flew by dropping leaflets! What a frenzy of joyful excitement rocked the village! One leaflet contained President Sergio Osmeña's proclamation that the Philippine Government had returned from exile. Osmeña had succeeded Manuel L. Quezon as President of the Commonwealth since the latter had passed away in the United States while the "good fight" was on. Another circular carried General MacArthur's announcement that the liberation forces were within striking distance of Manila.

In the midst of our excitement, our children unexpectedly came down with chicken pox. The disease attacked Andrew, Elsie, Dorcie, Cecilie, Betty, Arthur, Benny, Bachy, and even Boy. Our stay in Tigbi was prolonged.

On February 3, 1945, I was awakened by the sound of machine-gun fire from the northwest. I believed there was ground action near us and I sent Mang Genio to investigate.

"It is rumored the Americans have passed through Angat," Mang Genio reported later in the afternoon. Angat was only a few kilometers from us.

That night we saw columns of flame from the south. There was a crazy pattern of whizzing fireballs in the sky, like a dance of fairies. We presumed a landing in southern Luzon was under way, not knowing that Manila was a blazing inferno, touched off by the vengeance of a desperate enemy as it retreated.

# CHAPTER TWENTY-EIGHT

❦

## CRY NO MORE

*He maketh peace in
thy borders,
And filleth thee with
the finest of the wheat.*
Psalm 147:14

Tales of atrocities in the Ipo hilly region began to reach Tigbi, brought by refugees who passed the valley on their way to neighboring towns. "Some of the barrio people told me they had seen Mang Juan," Bayani reported to us excitedly.

We had been hoping that Sister Martha and her group would follow the trail taken by Mang Juan and the other survivors. The Japanese raid which followed Lily's return had forced us to leave Mang Genio's house in panicky haste, sending no word to our beloved friends.

In vain we waited for news.

Yang and I finally held a long conference with Bayani, Chung, and Mang Genio over the fate of Sister Martha and her group. "It is too late," Mang Genio concluded with a sigh. The situation then was such that nobody knew where they could be located and the military authorities were strictly banning civilians from crossing the battle lines.

We lingered in Tigbi for almost a month. We did not know that although the village was not fortified, it lay in a buffer zone where the anti-Japanese guerrillas and the pro-Japanese Makapilis (United Nippon Units) were both active. Anything could happen yet.

One night we heard noises outside the house—a commotion

among the villagers. Mang Genio immediately ran forth to greet a group of men. We were told they were friendly guerrillas, but, nevertheless, Mang Genio asked his relatives to caution us not to be seen.

> Behold, I send an Angel before thee, to keep thee in the way, and to bring thee into the place which I have prepared.
>
> Exodus 23:20

This message came to my wife in her daily reading. God was urging us to keep moving. Yang and I consulted Mang Genio. This time he shared our belief that we should go farther west. "Some people say the Americans have passed through the town of Santa Maria," the good farmer casually remarked. This was gladsome news, for we were not far from that town. Genio had a friend in Pulongbuhangin, a barrio along the highway a few miles from Santa Maria. The barrio was located a half day's walk west of Tigbi.

"But what about the children? They cannot walk as they did the last time. They are suffering from chicken pox," I told Mang Genio.

Our farmer friends had thought of that, too. "Tuya, Sabino, my three other relatives, and I shall carry the children to Pulong-buhangin," Mang Genio said. "We have prepared three litters. Two men will carry two children in one litter, and each litter can be covered with a cloth." The plan was both prudent and practical.

Six of our elder children were to ride in the litters. Yang would balance little Benny in a bamboo basket hanging from one end of a pole on his shoulders, with a basket of belongings hanging from the other end, while Amado would carry Andrew on his back. Boy would ride on the carabao and cover himself with an old raincoat. We had decided to make Pulongbuhangin our first stop on the way to Santa Maria.

As I was reading Psalm 147, I marveled to see this wonderful verse:

He maketh peace in
    thy borders,
And filleth thee with
    the finest of the wheat.

Psalm 147:14

Fine wheat! We had not tasted bread made of fine American wheat through the three years of Japanese occupation. "This is our go-signal to freedom," I said to the Yangs, the Chungs, and my wife, pointing to the Bible. "We are going to eat bread made of American wheat." They all smiled.

We asked Mang Genio to gather everybody for our journey into the new barrio. It was February 5, 1945. We sang our marching song, "Glory, Glory, Hallelujah"—a hymn we had sung nightly at our devotions since that desperate, rainy night of June 4, 1943, when our families had finally reached Ipo. Saying good-bye to Mang Genio's family and to all his relatives, we started the trek farther west. Across meadows and beside rice fields, the going was easy. By noon we had reached the highway. The village—Pulongbuhangin—was quiet. We saw no sign of the Americans.

"Look!" I yelled, pointing to huge tank tracks on both sides of the narrow road. "The enemy does not have tanks that big. The Americans must have passed here."

Suddenly Eva shouted, "Boxes! American paper boxes!" Louisa and Eva picked up all the candy and cigarette wrappers and empty ration cartons their arms could carry. When we reached the house of Mang Genio's friend, Eva discovered an unopened package of orange powder among the ration boxes. Like lightning, the children swarmed around her and then lined up. Each was given two teaspoonfuls of delicious orangeade.

The American forces had passed through this little barrio on their way to Santa Maria two days before. Overjoyed, we all sang "God Bless America!"

Now that we had reached Pulongbuhangin safely, Mang Sabino and three of his relatives bade farewell to us, leaving Mang Genio

184

and Mang Tuya behind to serve as our guide for the rest of the journey.

We gave our children two quiet nights' rest to regain their strength, and then continued westward. The sunny sky was smiling and the water shone like a crystal when we approached the Santa Maria River. I saw a Chinese swimming. He stared at me with knitted brows.

"Are you not Mr. Go?" he said in Chinese.

He was the first Chinese I had met outside of my own group in three years and one month. I wept, overcome.

"Cry no more, Mr. Go, the Americans have recaptured Manila. You can walk about confidently now," he said. Only then did we know that Manila had been liberated. The great event which we had looked forward to through the long months and years had now become a reality!

"As Noah came out from the ark, we are safe and free," I joyfully told the Yangs and my wife.

Of all that God had promised us, not one thing had been denied. I rejoiced to look at my wife and our children—Andrew, now five, Elsie six, Dorcie seven, Cecilie nine, and Betty ten. After three years of suffering and hardship, the children had grown tall and Fely was in robust health. Our faithful Louisa, who had cried once in despair, now realized that our hope had been fulfilled. And I had not failed my brother-in-law Amado by keeping him in the hills for safety.

I looked at Yang, Eva, and their children—Arthur and Benny. I knew they, too, were overwhelmed with thankfulness to God.

And the loyal, courageous Lily, the young, intelligent Eddie and Bayani, and steady, capable Mang Genio—God had certainly used them to serve His purpose best. Without their help, it would not have been possible for us to survive those interminable dark days in the jungle.

Bachy, Boy, Baby, and Chung had escaped with us from death to life. It was our fervent hope that their fathers and mothers and the rest of their families would all be liberated.

The story of Manila's liberation can be told in brief:

After the Sixth Army, under General Walter Krueger, landed at Lingayen Gulf and moved gradually southward to Manila, the Eighth Army, under General Robert Eichelberger, landed the Eleventh Airborne Division in Nasugbu, Batangas Province, in Southern Luzon. The Eleventh Paratroop Regiment was dropped behind the Japanese lines and occupied strategic Tagaytay Ridge, 36 miles south of Manila. It was immediately joined by the guerrillas.

The landing of the Eighth Army was given much publicity on the radio. Thus Yamashita rushed his troops and marines to the south, permitting a more rapid, unopposed American advance from the north. On the orders of General Walter Krueger the 37th Division, under General Robert S. Beightler, crossed the Pampanga river, cutting through Bulacan Province. It then joined General William C. Chase's First Cavalry Division at Plaridel, 26 miles north of Manila, which had arrived there through Nueva Ecija. The First Cavalry Division was an armored task force called the "Flying Squadron." The staccato sound of machine-gun fire, which we had heard when we were in Tigbi, was that of the First Cavalry units as they crushed enemy resistance in the Angat-Norzagaray area and rolled down through Santa Maria toward Manila. Nueva Ecija, Pampanga, and Bulacan are neighboring provinces in Central Luzon.

The morning of the fateful Saturday, February 3, 1945, dawned in Manila just like many mornings before it. American planes were greeted by heavy Japanese anti-aircraft fire. Though the booming of American guns could be heard in the distance, the buy-and-sell business in downtown Manila went on briskly as usual. The much inflated "Mickey Mouse" Japanese money was exchanged for market produce at an incredibly low rate. In the afternoon the First Cavalry tanks penetrated Grace Park, north of Manila. To avoid mines planted at the railroad crossing, they smashed through the stone wall of the San Lazaro railroad station. Guided by guerrillas under the leadership of Captain Manuel Colayco, who became the first casualty, the Tank Battalion rushed to the Santo Tomas internment camp. A tank named "Battling Basic" ploughed through the gate. The glorious First Cavalry had succeeded in its mission and liberated 3,251 internees at Santo Tomas, among them Sam Boyd Stagg, Roy Bennett and his family.

Manilans were electrified by the dramatic appearance of the American soldiers. Soon everyone was running wild in the streets, shouting "Victory Joe!" and making the "V" sign with his fingers. Sidewalk vendors rushed forward to offer the American soldiers *guinatan*—a native dish of camote, *gabe* (yams), and coconut milk—and whatever liquor was available. The American soldiers, in turn, tossed cigarettes and candy bars to the people.

By the time we were crossing the Santa Maria River, the fight was still raging in south Manila. However, communications had been resumed between north Manila and Santa Maria, the town we were entering.

The Chinese we had seen swimming in the Santa Maria River and who had greeted me with the news of the liberation of Manila courteously introduced himself as Ang Tun Siu, brother of the principal of the Anglo-Chinese school in Manila. "For three long years you have upheld your loyalty. It will be a joy for our people in Manila to know you are safe," he said. He offered his services to make contacts in the city for us. He had a bicycle, the best means of transportation at the time.

I was touched. After three dark years, the first countryman I met had recognized me.

We asked Ang to look up the *Fookien Times* people in Manila. Cheerfully, he bade us good-bye and promised to return to us in Santa Maria.

Though right in the path of the American cavalry, Santa Maria had been miraculously spared the ravages of war. The Japanese, for once, had not put up a fight there. The whole town celebrated for days.

Mang Genio rented a small bungalow with furniture and a real kitchen, which delighted our women after years of primitive housekeeping. Since Santa Maria was an egg-producing town, the children no longer had to lick egg shells but could have as many eggs as they wanted. They enjoyed hearty meals at last and soon recovered fully from chicken pox. There was a public pool with a hot spring, where our children bathed to their heart's content. It was exhilarating to breathe the free air.

# CHAPTER TWENTY-NINE

❧❧❧

## DUST AND ASHES

*Go thou thy way till the end be;*
*for thou shalt rest, and stand in*
*thy lot at the end of the days.*
Daniel 12:13

The first American soldier we met was Ran Warthen, a radio man of the First Cavalry. "As I shake hands with you, my hunted life ends," I greeted him. Warthen was a likeable young man. When he told us he had to leave town next day to rejoin his unit in Manila, we invited him to our bungalow and the children sang American songs for him. We were impressed by his sincerity and friendliness, and he was touched by our three years' experiences.

Next to move in was the 112th Cavalry, the Texas National Guard under the command of Colonel Clyde Grand, a fine Christian soldier. He looked with amazement on my press pass issued on December 15, 1941 by MacArthur's Headquarters. We recommended Guerrilla Lieutenant Tuya to him as a man who could give the American forces detailed geographic information on the Ipo area. Everyone could foresee that the battle to crack the Yamashita Line would be furious.

Some officers of the 112th Cavalry dined with us. They brought corned beef, pork and beans, and other canned goods. We were giving the party, but judging by the gusto and relish with which we ate, it seemed to have been given for us. "We can't see how you can eat those canned goods as if they were the most delicious food on earth," a soldier remarked. We told them we had not tasted food like that for three years. The officer, in turn, heartily dug into the native food we offered. They had had corned beef and pork and beans for months. The fresh fish, fried chicken, and fresh vegetables were as delicious to them as the canned goods were to us.

Great was our joy in entertaining them, for they were our liberators, angels sent to redeem us. "Even though we went through hardships all the way from the jungle of New Guinea to the Philippines, we now realize it was worth it," said the officer.

The same day we had reached Santa Maria General MacArthur had passed through on his way to Manila with Carlos P. Romulo, now a general, and General Le Grand Diller, the major who was MacArthur's spokesman and who had signed my press pass at MacArthur's Headquarters in 1941. Diller later wrote me: "Even in far-off Australia we learned that the Japanese had closed your paper and we were not surprised. Those were difficult times for all of us and particularly for you, who were not only living in a country occupied by the enemy but were men whom the enemy would have liked to eliminate."

"I am a little late. But we finally came," said General MacArthur when, choking with emotion, he addressed the cheering crowd in Manila. The last act of the Japanese troops before retreating from Manila was to set fire to the city. Flames raged for days.

"The *Fookien Times* plant was burned down. Nothing is left but ashes," Ang Tun Siu sadly reported when he had returned to Santa Maria from the city. Then he handed me a one-sheet copy of the *Fookien Times!* Our loyal co-workers had banded together and, with the help of a small printing shop, had put out the *Fookien Times* on February 8, 1945. This was a great day for me. My newspaper had resumed publication.

"God gives and God takes, praised be the Lord," I told Ang. He had fulfilled his mission well. Cheerful once more, he bade us good-bye.

Anxious to be back with my newspaper, I left with Yang for Manila. The rest of our group was to follow later. Shells whizzed over our heads. Ashes from the city fires blew thick like a desert sandstorm. Columns of smoke swirled sky-high. Three years before, I had seen the black smoke of Pandacan district foreshadowing our dark days. Now I saw the mad dreams of the Japanese militarists who had sought to conquer Asia disperse with the dust and ashes.

As Yang and I faced the conflagration, we could see Mary Stagg, Hawthorne Darby, Helen Wilk, and other martyrs—their faces outshining the flames' brilliance. Freedom was ours once more, and theirs were not vain sacrifices. Twelve years later, the three lady missionaries were to receive posthumously the award of the Philippine Legion of Honor—the highest Philippine honor ever given to American ladies—by President Magsaysay, the one-time guerrilla leader who almost suffered martyrdom with them during the war.

To my delight, a good friend and an old colleague, Frederick S. Marquardt—now editor of the *Arizona Republic* in Phoenix, who had forecast in his book that I would be a goner during the Japanese occupation—was serving the U.S. Armed Forces as Chief of the Office of War Information. He was then right in town. Marquardt described Manila during those hectic days and our reunion as follows: *

> Well, it was dangerous and it was discouraging. People got killed in the shelling and sniping and people starved to death quite literally even in Sto. Tomas where the food came too late for some. Few people had homes and there was barely enough housing to go around and virtually everyone had lost almost everything he owned. No family came through that tragic liberation without at least losing one member.
>
> It was war at its worst—and yet there was something magnificent about seeing one of the world's great historic cities shake its fists at the fates and begin to dig out of the rubble. In the muck and the dust and the blood and hunger there was an exaltation of spirit that seemed to be saying . . . this City, this Christian

* From "A Cable Came While I Was Covering a UN Meeting," 1948 Fookien Times Yearbook.

City, this lone Christian capital in the Orient is made of greater stuff than anyone ever dreamed of.

And then there was one I will never forget. He was Go Puan Seng, publisher of the *Fookien Times,* who came in from the hills around Ipo where he had played hide-and-seek with the Japanese. He proudly exhibited his press pass issued by MacArthur's Headquarters in December 1941. "What can I do for you, Fritz?" he asked.

I was flabbergasted. I had been eating regularly, was well-clothed, held a good job with the government of the United States, and here he was, walking out of the jungle and wanting to help me! I gave him some magazines to read, chocolate bars for his kids, and an apple for Mrs. Go. Then suddenly it dawned on me that he could help.

"Come on over to Carmelo and Bauermann," I said. We walked over—there was no other way there—and I showed him where the Japanese had dumped all the Japanese types out of racks on the floor. "We've to print leaflets in Japanese," I said. "How can I get those types put back in the racks where they belong?"

"Simple," said Go, and headed in the direction of Binondo. A couple of hours later, he and his assistant were back with ten Chinese printers. They could read Japanese characters which are, of course, really Chinese. In a few days they had cleaned up the mess, redistributed the types and were setting them for a paper we called the *Bakkassan Shimbun* or "Parachute News." Hundreds of thousands of copies of it were dropped on the enemy, and the printing was so good that some Japanese thought Tokyo had fallen. "You couldn't print such a fine Japanese paper anywhere but in Tokyo," they told our interpreters.

To our great joy and amazement, Aqui, Tito, and Samuel Huang had been saved by the timely arrival of the Eighth Army.

*192*

With the help of guerrillas, the Eighth Army had liberated the internees at Los Baños, 40 miles south of Manila, and had then rushed to Muntinglupa and saved the lives of many political prisoners in the state prison there. The Japanese soldiers had marked many of them for revenge, and had already slaughtered some.

Tito hiked with Aqui from Muntinglupa to south Manila and there found Sister Rosario alive in the backyard of their ruined house, which had been hit by shells. Sister Rosario, in her moment of distress, had come across the following Bible verse:

Though I have afflicted thee,
I will afflict thee no more.

Nahum 1:12

True to the promise, Tito came back to her. And when the two found their Bachy safe and well, they wept with joy. With Dr. Darby and Miss Wilk gone, Tito was elected to the general managership of the Emmanuel Hospital to work for its post-war rehabilitation, the very hospital in whose isolation room I took refuge upon my return to Manila when the Japanese Army was hot hunting for me in March, 1942.

Aqui also had found his house destroyed. South Manila was a shambles. While he was comforted that Boy, Baby, and Chung were alive, he was shocked to learn that his wife and a great number of his family had not come out from the hilly region.

Determined though he was, Aqui could not enter Ipo to search for them. The battle was heavy. He was told to wait for the outcome.

Then Mario came. He had escaped with Mang Jore's son from the inferno of the Blue Mountains. Under cover of darkness, they had sneaked through thorns and bushes, inching their way and crawling in the ditches like snakes so as to evade the Japanese soldiers.

"What happened to Sister Martha after she left us?" I asked Mario.

"We moved from Camp Hope to Mang Jore's and from Mang

Jore's eastward to the Blue Mountains. The retreating Japanese caught up with us," Mario said. "Impo and Becky were caught by them in a camote farm. I heard Becky screaming."

Explosions of bombs rent the air on all sides; machine guns and rifles cracked intermittently. Desperate Japanese soldiers, hungry and exhausted, ran wild and mad. Mario dared not rush to Becky's rescue nor go anywhere near the camote farm.

"Possibly Becky and Impo were both being killed," was the only guess Mario could make.

Poor Becky—she never knew that her husband had died in Manila from privation shortly before liberation!

"I was frightened by the cruelty of the soldiers and ran away with Mang Jore's son," Mario continued.

"What about Sister Martha and the rest of the family?" I persisted.

"The children were hungry, and they were sick most of the time. It was hard to move the whole group," Mario replied. So they had all been trapped inside the battle lines.

Poor children! Poor Priscilla, Amelia, Linda, Eddie, and Boying!

"But what about Ernesto?" I questioned again.

"Ernesto stayed with his mother," Mario said.

Ernesto Aquino, the faithful and brave young man, had no heart to leave by himself and must have stayed to suffer with his mother and sisters, I thought. And I presumed, their poor maid, Gorgonia, too.

A former Philippine scout, Mario soon joined the American Army through the arrangement I made with Marquardt.

From Apogan Pass to Ipo Dam, the Japanese troops held the Yamashita Line despite heavy American bombing and shelling. The jungle had become a roaring inferno.

When the American forces and the guerrillas finally penetrated the rocky pass, Aqui immediately entered Ipo together with Mang Genio and a searching party. Hill after hill they climbed and explored, ranging over every square foot, hoping against hope.

"For ten days and nights," Aqui told me, "I subsisted on meager rations and slept under the trees. I searched everywhere for Martha and the children. I stepped over corpses and stumbled on, mile after mile, until I reached a foothill of the Blue Mountains. There I found clothes belonging to my family hanging on a tree. My heart gave a great bound, and almost delirious with joy, I called and called to them, but there was no answer. I kept shouting their names, one by one, but only the hills echoed my voice. They were gone."

I recalled the last verse in Daniel:

> Go thou thy way till the end be; for thou shalt rest, and stand in thy lot at the end of the days.
>
> Daniel 12:13

"This was the promise Sister Martha received in the first hour of 1944," I told Aqui. "We all had an uneasy feeling for her then, but we can be comforted now. For by that promise, Sister Martha is now at rest and is waiting for her reward."

> And we know that all things work together for good to them that love God, to them who are the called according to his purpose.
>
> Romans 8:28

# CHAPTER THIRTY

ఆర్ప

## SOWING THE SEEDS OF FREEDOM

> *Verily, verily I say unto you, except a corn of wheat fall into the ground to die, it abides alone: but if it dies, it bringeth forth much fruit.*
>
> John 12:24

The lush green jungle, once covering heights and valleys, had been wiped out in battle fire. Many a life had perished in the flames with the bushes and the trees. Many a home had joined the ashes and the dust. The sighs of the unchanging wind breathed eternal lament for the days that would not return.

Aqui, who became Secretary-Treasurer of the Philippine Amateur Athletic Federation, the athletic center of the country, after the war, had rebuilt his house in Ipo. Every weekend he goes to the hills to steep himself in the past—the past which can neither come back to him nor yet be taken away.

Eddie, who visited the ruins of Mang Genio's farm in Ipo, found my manuscript, composed of random notes and essays in Chinese and English, still intact in its kerosene can, still wrapped in the old canvas bag. However, it was not lying where Lily had hidden it, in the bushes beside the brook, on the day the Japanese soldiers had raided Mang Genio's house. It stood on a huge rock in the middle of the stream! Had it remained in the bushes, it would have been burned when the hills were razed to the ground. Had it fallen into the stream, it would not only have gotten wet but also would have been swept away by the current. But miraculously, it had fallen on a huge rock lying in the middle of the stream, where neither fire nor water could reach or damage it. It had, indeed, come safely through—the precious raw material which served as germ for this story.

In the 1,105 trying days—from December 31, 1941 to January 9, 1945—there was not a single day that I was not imperiled. I lived by days, by hours, by moments. None would have given me a chance in a thousand to survive the war.

From the day I left home to tread the road of an exile, armed only with the faith that God would be my sun and my shield, I firmly believed that during the Japanese occupation I would have to undergo a tremulous life—just as when strong winds rent the mountain, the earth trembled, and fire flared when Elisha was a wanted man, fleeing from his powerful enemies. But I also firmly believed that I would overcome hazardous tribulations and live to hear the still, small voice of God.

I had overcome the impossibilities, going in and out of Manila while the Japanese were in hot pursuit. I did not ask the Lord to turn night into day, as Joshua had when he prayed that the sun hold still at Gibeon and the moon stay in the valley of Aijalon; mine was to have witnessed the wonders of how prayer transformed the worn-out nags beneath a stormy sky into galloping horses climbing the steep cliffs under a starry heaven, carrying us through a most dangerous journey.

Many a time we had escaped death when the Japanese scouting soldiers were as close as a hair's breadth to us. But we, too, marvelled at God's miraculous protection; we remembered that in the days of old when the enemy hunting for Elisha reached Dothan, their eyes became blurred and they were led to Samaria instead.

We were caught inside the enemy's cordon on the eve of the great battle, dangerous just as St. Paul's ship had been at the mercy of a raging sea between Crete and A'dria. Neither sun nor stars appeared for many a day and fearful was the tempest. But St. Paul did not abandon hope. Neither did we fear for a moment that God would forsake us.

During the last phase of the war, when the Japanese soldiers were searching our grass house—if the mountains had toppled over, we could not have been more shocked than we were by this dangerous encounter—we found solace in St. Augustine, who once said, "The moment God seems to be farthest is, actually, the moment He is nearest."

There were times when I pondered my fate and that of Mother Stagg, Dr. Darby, Miss Wilk, Mrs. Martha Aquino, and other martyrs and friends. I meditated and immersed myself in the good Book of St. John, in which Jesus told Peter, "When you were young, you girded yourself and walked where you would; but when you are old, you will stretch out your hands, and another will gird you and carry you where you do not wish to go." Peter saw John and said to Jesus, "Lord, what about this man?" Jesus said to him, "If it is my will that he remain until I come, what is that to you? Follow me." There are Peters; there are Johns. Peter died on the cross. John lived to testify. Living and dying, they were one in faith.

> *And every virtue we possess*
> *And every victory won,*
> *And every thought of holiness*
> *Are His alone.*

Harriet Auber

It was in February, 25 years ago, that I had left Santa Maria with Yang. We had ridden in an army car together with the officers of the American cavalry. With us were the bodies of American soldiers who had fought and died at the Norzagaray-Ipo front. At the graveyard we saw many more bodies awaiting interment. "They are yesterday's casualties," we were told. What about the lives lost during the heavy battle and long campaign that had led up to this—yesterday's casualties and those of yesterday's yesterdays?

When a general achieves victory, lo! thousands of skulls bleach in the sun.

Chinese Adage

Yang and I stood silently as their bodies were lowered from the army car.

> Verily, verily I say unto you, except a corn of wheat
> fall into the ground to die, it abides alone: but if it
> dies, it bringeth forth much fruit.
>
> John 12:24

We were not merely burying the dead, but sowing the very seeds of freedom. These were my thoughts then.

Now, a quarter of a century has passed. We have come to their Memorial to pay our homage, together with the First Cavalry's famed commanding general who fought with them. "They die unquestioning, uncomplaining, with faith in their hearts, and on their lips, the hope that we would go on to victory. Their fame and their name have been the birthright of every child born in freedom." These words of tribute were paid them by General MacArthur in a speech delivered on the grounds of his old battlefield during his last visit to the Philippines.

As the noonday sun moved slowly toward the west and the gentle swaying leaves and branches spread an increasing shade, we left the Memorial. The two young American soldiers from Vietnam waved farewell and lingered on.